STRATEGY ACTIVATION

How to Turn Your Vision into Marketplace Success

Scott Glatstein

This publication is designed to educate and provide general information regarding the subject matter covered. While the author has taken reasonable precautions in the preparation of this book, and believes the facts presented within the book are accurate, neither the publisher nor author assumes any responsibility for errors and omissions. The author and publisher specifically disclaim any liability resulting from the use or application of the information contained in this book.

Library of Congress Control Number: 2007943553

Publisher's Cataloging-in-Publication
(Provided by Quality Books, Inc.)

Glatstein, Scott.
   Strategy activation : keeping promises to the
marketplace / Scott Glatstein.
     p. cm.
     Includes index.
     LCCN 2007943553
     ISBN-13: 978-0-9801649-2-3
     ISBN-10: 0-9801649-2-3

     1. Strategic planning. 2. Industrial management.
I. Title.

HD30.28.G53 2008   658.4
                  QBI08-600009

Printed in the United States of America on acid-free paper.

To my Dad for showing me how to lead
with integrity, compassion and generosity.

TABLE
OF CONTENTS

ACKNOWLEDGEMENTS

I t shouldn't surprise anyone that the concepts and tools presented in this book were not developed in a vacuum. Over the years the notion of Strategy Activation has been debated, molded, and nurtured by friends, relatives, colleagues, and clients. In addition, other authors…leaders in the fight to link execution to strategy…influenced our thinking and inspired us to join the battle. In particular, I am grateful to Larry Bossidy & Ram Charan (*Execution*), Lawrence Hrebiniak (*Making Strategy Work*) and Robert Kaplan & David Norton (*The Strategy-Focused Organization*) for blazing that trail.

I want to thank Lisa Zakrajsek, John Hetterick, and John Pierson for their continuing friendship and unwavering encouragement.

I want to thank my colleagues Alan Bergstrom, Chris Westphal and Tina Uphoff for helping shape the Strategy Activation concept and process. I also want to thank them for their literary contributions and suffering through the early drafts of the manuscript.

I want to thank Rachel Wegscheid for assisting with the book cover design, the website and all of the marketing activities surrounding the launch of the book.

I want to thank Mahesh Grossman, Brian O'Connell and The Authors Team for their help in organizing this work

And I want to thank Ellen, my wife and partner for 22 years, for always believing in me. This book and more importantly, IMPERATIVES, LLC, would never have happened without your support and unbounded optimism. Thank you for being a wonderful part of my life.

WHY STRATEGIES FAIL

"Strategies are intellectually simple; their execution is not."
—Larry Bossidy, author of *Execution: The Discipline of Getting Things Done*

"If you don't know where you're going,
you could wind up somewhere else,"
—Yogi Berra

T here's an old Harvard Business School adage that theory stands a much better chance of success than execution. The line is as relevant now as it was 50 years ago.

All it means is that the best-laid plans can go awry once exposed to the light of day and the rudeness and ruthlessness of reality.

Former President Lyndon Johnson understood that. He often told a story of a man who had applied for a job as a flagman at a railroad crossing. The man was told he'd be handed the job if he could pass a test consisting of just a single question

The applicant was told to imagine that he was a flagman at a crossing consisting of a single track when he suddenly observed the *Continental Express* bearing down from the east at 95 miles per hour and, coming from the other direction, the *Century Limited* at 100 miles per hour. With the trains only 500 yards apart, the man was asked, what would he do under such a circumstance? Without hesitation, the would-be flagman responded that he would go and get his brother-in-law.

Puzzled, the railroad examiner inquired, "What good would that do?"

The job applicant promptly replied, "He ain't never seen a train wreck."

Clearly the would-be flagman didn't understand the overarching strategy of his potential employer (prevent accidents) nor his potential role in executing that strategy. Unfortunately, this is not unlike the current state of corporate execution as evidenced by the train wrecks we see everyday in the marketplace.

How would I know? Well, my name is Scott Glatstein and I develop corporate strategy execution practices for a living. In fact, I've been doing so, as a corporate executive and a consultant, for 25 years.

In that time I've learned a thing or two about strategy execution – what works and what doesn't. I've learned that organizations who have mastered the intricacies of strategy execution are, far and away, more likely to outperform competitors in key areas like revenue growth, profitability and customer satisfaction. I've also learned that strategic plans often fail when burdened by managers who lack the skills necessary to manage strategic execution campaigns. They also fail when there are no ingrained processes to guide strategic execution or inadequate tools necessary to enable success.

The good news is that, from what I've witnessed on the front lines, strategy execution can improve as executives streamline daily activities and realign them so they are in harmony with business goals.

There is more good news: after decades of neglect, top managers are becoming increasingly aware of the importance of strategy execution. According to a recent study by the Conference Board, strategy execution ranks high in the top ten "challenges" facing senior managers (strategic execution, in fact, ranked third out of 91 potential challenges, the Conference Board reported).

That mindset won't change anytime soon. *Strategy+Business* magazine reports that strategic execution is the number one issue facing senior managers over the next ten years.

THE AGE OF STRATEGY ACTIVATION

So what's all the hoopla about? Why is strategy execution the next "must have" business discipline today? How can businesses leverage solid marketplace execution of strategic vision to fatten their bottom lines *and* set the stage for future growth and prosperity?

Good questions all, and ones that I will spend the following ten chapters answering.

I'll spend a good chunk of the book examining what has gone so wrong with strategy execution practices. It's not a pretty picture. Studies show that nine out of ten business strategies are poorly implemented in the marketplace. In fact, poor execution is the number one reason businesses fail. While there are many issues that drive poor execution, they all seem to point to a common factor: a lack of preparedness to implement the strategy that has been created.

David Norton, author and professor at Harvard Business School, tells us that only 10 percent of all business strategies are effectively implemented. Companies invest so much time and energy into developing the perfect stratagem, yet 90 percent fail. This is rarely due to a strategy's inherent ineffectiveness. Poor marketplace execution of the plan is often the culprit. That should be a wake-up call for all business executives.

Fortunately, there is a solution that meets all of a strategic manager's needs, goals, and expectations, one that most people don't know about. Its name is the title that graces the cover of this book – Strategy Activation.

> Strategy Activation is a business process that my company has designed to address the gap between strategy creation and marketplace implementation. It focuses simultaneously on all the key success factors necessary in creating successful corporate strategy execution programs.
>
> Strategy Activation recognizes that your company's over-arching strategy is a promise – a promise made to the marketplace and to the customers whose day-to-day experiences with the organization's products and services – determines the ultimate success of the business. Strategy Activation is the new bridge that spans the chasm between executive-level strategic intent and organization-wide marketplace execution. It takes *what* an organization wants to do and defines *how* it is going to do it. It ensures that the promise made to the marketplace is driven by every employee across every customer touchpoint every day.

WHY STRATEGIES FAIL

I'll go into greater detail later on in this book, but for background purposes, there are four primary reasons why a company can't effectively implement its strategies:

1) The strategy fails to recognize the limitations of the existing organization.

Strategy makes huge demands on an organization's capabilities and resources. While an organization can certainly transform its capabilities over time, there is a limit to how far and how fast. Recognizing what the organization can realistically deliver before launching in a new direction is essential.

2) Employees don't know how the strategy applies to their daily work.

Many companies don't communicate strategy broadly or effectively. If the strategy is to offer world-class customer service, what does that really mean? What does it mean to the salesperson on the street, to the customer service representative in the call center, and to the marketing manager at headquarters? When employees don't know how the strategy affects their everyday work, they aren't likely to implement it properly.

3) The organization's business systems or processes can't support the strategy.

It's difficult to implement a new strategy without changing the way the organization works. Does the way in which work flows across departments and divisions support the marketplace intent? Can the systems and tools meet the demands of the new strategic vision? Pursuing a new strategy with old capabilities is a recipe for disaster.

4) Performance metrics and rewards are not aligned with the strategy.

An organization may communicate, for example, that it wants to develop strong, ongoing customer partnerships, but instead it rewards short-term revenues over long-term profits (thereby giving little incentive for individual managers to place emphasis on establishing longer-term and more profitable client relationships).

A SAAB STORY

The answer to these problems lies in "activating" the strategy and thus creating an organization that is ready, willing and able to bring your strategic vision to market.

Specifically, as I'll show inside these pages, organizations need to go beyond articulating the typical strategic plan. They must translate their strategy into specific employee roles and create the infrastructure and processes that enable them to fulfill those prescribed roles.

For an exemplary example, consider Swedish carmaker, Saab. Despite a long history of industry engineering and design innovations in safety, comfort and performance, Saab's market impact was fading – to the tune of seven straight unprofitable years and a noticeable loss of market share in the crowded luxury car market. It became clear that the fabled carmaker had lost its way. Annual strategy shifts, each designed to prop up the business, left consumers, dealers and employees confused and uninspired.

At around this time, Saab undertook a robust research effort among high end car buyers and uncovered a heretofore unrecognized insight into Saab's core customers -. Saab owners are fiercely individualistic. They pride themselves on breaking from the pack and taking the road less traveled. And because of that, they demand an individualized customer experience that is unique and unconventional.

To create the new and unique experience their customers hungered for, Saab fashioned a new management position – VP, Brand Experience and Management. This elevated the importance of the holistic customer experience.

Five guiding principles were identified to provide an internal compass for the organization and drive the optimal experience. A cross-functional Brand Council was chartered to ensure that these principles were internalized and adhered to across the organization.

Saab also recognized that their new strategy required real change throughout the organization. To realign employee behavior and corporate culture Saab created internal brand workshops: All 16,000 employees were trained through *Saab Way* orientations. In addition, performance measurement systems were retooled and incentives and rewards established for meeting new customer experience objectives.

As the guiding principles took hold, many real changes in the existing customer experience started to take shape, including the following:

- Unique interior and exterior physical design cues emerged that differentiated the Saab from the rest of the luxury cars on the market.
- Lease and purchase programs were customized and tailored to individual customer needs.
- An annual Saab Owners Convention provided opportunities for loyal Saab followers to meet with corporate executives, attend special car clinics, and get a sneak-peek at new products and programs in development.
- Saab Magazine was launched, featuring lifestyle articles such as wine & cooking, travel, health & fitness that appealed to the "off the beaten path" tastes of Saab owners.
- Showrooms were redesigned and a new no-pressure consultative sales approach was developed.
- Some dealers even provided at-home or at-office test drives.

Perhaps the most visible and intriguing change came in after-sales service. To provide the individualized experience envisioned by the strategy, Saab executives conceived a whole new series of tools to enable its servicing crews and reinforce the Saab experience at this critical customer touchpoint.

It began at the point of manufacture. Each new Saab rolling off the assembly line received a unique bar code placed in the windshield of the car. This bar code linked to a master database that maintained the car's ownership data and servicing records. Many dealerships (those focused on customer service and retention) were equipped with handheld units that read the bar code, accessed the database, and displayed the car's record.

As a customer drove his or her car in for servicing, the waiting technician scanned the bar code. Before the customer exited the vehicle, the handheld unit displayed the customer's name and recent service record. Thus the technician could greet the customer as follows:

"Welcome back, Mrs. Smith. How is your day going so far? I see the last time you were in we adjusted your brakes. Did that clear up the issue you were having? It seems today you're here for an oil change and lube.

"Are there any other concerns you'd like us to look at while the car is here?"

Not only did this interaction create the individualized *experience* that Saab owners yearn for, it minimized the distrust that typically exists between car owner and mechanic. This personalized treatment helped solidify the bond between the customer and the dealership, thus increasing customer loyalty and retention. This service would not be possible, however, without the technology and tools Saab provided to its service technicians.

Saab recognized that developing a compelling marketplace promise is just a first step. It all comes down to the customer's actual experience with the organization. That's what determines the ultimate success of a strategy. Thus, before launching a new strategy, whether it is service-centric, price-driven, luxury-focused, or some other viable approach, an organization must align the people, the processes and the systems to the customer experience it seeks to achieve.

In the first year post-implementation of their new strategy, Saab saw unit sales increase 55%. Awareness of the Saab brand increased 30%. Consideration among potential buyers increased 72% and inquires per month rose 179%. All of this was accomplished as incentive spending declined 67%.

That same year its competitors experienced flat or negative sales growth resulting in a nice share bump for Saab.

Saab recognized that developing a compelling marketplace promise is just a first step. It all comes down to the customer's actual experience with the organization. That's what determines the ultimate success of a strategy.

Thus, before launching a new strategy, whether it is service-centric, price-driven, luxury-focused, or some other viable approach, an organization must align the people, the processes and the systems to the customer experience it seeks to achieve.

That, as I prove in this book, is where Strategy Activation comes into play.

Inside these pages, I'll take you on a journey, one where as you come out the other side, you'll realize that the relationship between theory and execution has been changed forever – and that Strategy Activation is the reason why.

In short, you'll recognize that having the knowledge and capabilities essential to create, implement and manage your own Strategy Activation initiatives aren't a luxury.

They're the new business imperatives.

CHAPTER ONE

TURNING GOOD INTENTIONS INTO PROFITS

[Alice came to a fork in the road and saw
the Cheshire Cat in a tree. Alice asks the cat:]
"Would you tell me, please, which way I ought to go from here?"
"That depends a good deal on where you want to go," said the Cat.
"It doesn't much matter where," said Alice.
"Then it doesn't matter which way you go," said the Cat.
– From Lewis Carroll's *Alice in Wonderland*

Okay, let's get the bad news out of the way first.

Nine out of ten business strategies fail.

Surprised? Don't be. Statistics point to the hard truth that even strategies diligently planned around the latest trends and reports, fashioned with the most obvious market opportunities and solid competitive analysis in mind, don't often equate to market traction and an improved bottom line.

That's daunting news, but it's also a tremendous wake-up call.

Bringing strategies to life is not an easy task, but it is what makes all the difference. In this chapter – indeed in this book – we'll examine the many reasons why business strategies fail and what distinguishes higher performing companies from lower performing ones.

When many companies look to improve their value proposition or upgrade their product line, they think hard about how they will communicate those goals, but forget about how they will actually achieve them. So, designing strategies is only the first step in a series of necessary actions.

Think about it this way: business strategy directly communicates a company's intent to the public. The intent of course must be meaningful or attractive to the audience. If you follow through on delivering valued intentions, you will create profits, reinforce your brand, and, most importantly, persuade customers that you will make good on your word. But if you fail to come through, you're communicating the opposite message to the marketplace.

Strategy Activation *means the difference between keeping your strategies locked on track versus losing your way.*

ROOTS OF STRATEGY ACTIVATION

The American Management Association (AMA) commissioned the Human Resource Institute (HRI) to conduct a literature review and a global survey focusing on the execution of strategy. Within this study, the research team defined *strategy* as "*a major plan that an organization makes to attain a defined and positive business goal,*" and it defined *strategy execution* as "*The process of implementing such plans and achieving such goals.*" Of course, getting from strategy to successful implementation requires more than simple intent.

The key translation process called *Strategy Activation* must be inserted between a firm's conceptual strategic designs and the actual execution in order to succeed in the marketplace. Strategy Activation is about transformation (of a strategy) into identifiable, desired activities and alignment (of the organization) to enable those activities to be realized. Properly applied, it both prepares and leads an organization to successfully implement its plans. In short, Strategy Activation takes "what" an organization wants to do and defines "how" it is going to do it.

The process defines each employee's roles and responsibilities and ensures he or she has the necessary training that will yield success within the context of proposed strategies. It also matches rewards systems to the behaviors the organization must reinforce. Finally, it requires ensuring that the tools and the workflow processes enable employees to accomplish their defined goals. In short, your employees need clear direction and the infrastructure to support them. These are the levers that will "activate" your strategy.

A Fortune Magazine study has shown that seven out of ten CEOs who fail do so not because of bad strategy, but because of bad execution.

So, let's get back to the statistic; why do so many business strategies fail to achieve their goals? Who or what gets in the way of building an industry-leading, go-to-market strategy or a winning new product strategy?

While companies might find it tempting to place the blame on the strategy itself or fault its employees, such scapegoats are merely symptoms of a systemic disease.

The fault has far more to do with *how little* businesses strive to align their new strategies with the internal systems they already have in place. Those systems include internal staff goals, business systems, and everyday processes. Consequently, that's exactly what Strategy Activation entails – rethinking goals and business systems in terms of the proposed strategy.

Historically, work has been divided into two parts: strategy and execution. Top executives wrote the strategy (which always looked good on paper) and everyone else was supposed to execute it. However, many necessary steps and important questions were usually skipped over in between theory and actualization. Can the company execute its strategy within its existing culture, reward system, or fundamental workflow processes? Would employees be able to implement the strategy given the new expectations placed on their performance?

To further demonstrate the point, think about the following scenario: Would it seem logical to have one person plan a dinner party menu while another person is responsible for both the food budget and the shopping? What if they didn't coordinate their activities beforehand? You can imagine the implications if the first person invited the neighbors to a gourmet meal, while the second person simply shopped for beer and cold cuts as usual. This simple example demonstrates what happens when planning and execution aren't linked together. It is not simply a communication issue. Perhaps the first person has no idea of the costs and time required to actually create such an extravagant meal. Maybe the second person does not even know what gourmet food looks like or lacks the requisite cooking skills. In either case, it makes no sense to invite the neighbors (or even decide which neighbors to invite) until you know what kind of dinner can realistically be provided or what changes both people need to make in order for the gourmet dream to become a reality.

In more recent years, authors like Ken Bossidy and Ram Charan (*Execution: The Discipline of Getting Things Done*) and Lawrence Hrebiniak (*Making Strategy Work*) have helped break down the historical wall that exists between strategy and execution. However, in most organizations, the gap between strategy development and strategy implementation still remains.

WHY STRATEGIES FAIL

As a business culture, we have planted the seeds for imbalance early on, often in some of our most important institutions. Take business schools. Even prestigious schools like Wharton or Harvard tend to overemphasize strategy development at the expense of formal training on how to make strategy successful. As a result, many managers learn about strategy execution in the school of hard knocks. Even then, some managers never learn why their strategies continue to fail. We further validate this emphasis on strategy by promoting the best "strategic thinkers" over those who merely execute well in the marketplace.

The good news is that things are changing, helped by thorough examinations of why things go awry. What we've seen is there are a few fundamental reasons why strategies fail. In understanding them we can build a better, stronger platform for success.

With that thought in mind, let's take a look at the four primary reasons why strategies might not be living up to their full profit potential.

1) **The strategy fails to recognize the limitations of the existing organization.**

   Marketplace strategy makes huge demands on an organization's capabilities and resources. While your organization can certainly transform its capabilities over time, there is a limit to how far and how fast. Recognizing what your organization *can* realistically deliver before crafting a new direction is essential to your business success.

2) Employees don't know how the strategy applies to their daily work.

Many companies don't communicate strategy clearly or effectively enough to their employees. If, for example, your strategy is to offer the best service, what does that really mean? What does it mean to your salesperson on the street, to your customer service representative in the call center and to your marketing manager at headquarters? If your employees don't know how the "go-to-market" strategy affects their everyday work, they aren't likely to implement it properly.

3) The organization's business systems or processes can't support the strategy.

It's difficult to implement a new strategy without changing the way the organization works on a daily basis. Does the way in which work flows across your various departments and divisions support your marketplace intent? Can your systems and tools meet the demands of the new strategic vision? Remember that pursuing a new strategy with old capabilities is a recipe for disaster.

4) Performance metrics and rewards are not aligned with the strategy.

If your organization strives to be a service leader but is instead rewarding its customer service reps for keeping calls short (whether or not this leads to the resolution of a customer's problem), there may be a disconnect between performance metrics and the communicated strategy. Do reward systems and business strategies make sense in terms of the strategy and overall goal? Are you creating measurement tools that make employees feel good about their performance but don't really gauge the company's key success factors? Metrics and rewards must always be aimed at the specific employee behaviors sought – behaviors that support your company's strategic vision.

In a London Times study of 1,000 companies, 80 percent of directors said they had the right strategies but only 14 percent thought they were implementing them well.

All four of these issues share one common theme: your organization's preparedness to implement the "go-to-market" strategy you have just created. Strategy has to be more than a feel-good presentation shared with your managers, shareholders and the media. It has to be woven into the fabric of your organization.

If, for example, a company publicly unveils a new and improved customer service leadership strategy, it is making a concrete promise – a promise that conveys what the organization intends to deliver to its customers and the marketplace. Strategy execution determines whether an organization can turn good intentions into real profits.

In the study I mentioned earlier, the AMA/HRI team specifically wanted to find out what drives execution. They also wanted to isolate significant differences in how higher performing and lower performing organizations execute their strategies. Therefore, they sought to identify which companies – based on self-reports – are best at strategy execution and which excel in the areas of revenue growth, market share, profitability, and customer satisfaction. Although it is impossible to fully attribute causality in any survey, the data suggest that some approaches to execution are more valuable than others and that higher performers use those strategies to a greater extent than lower performers.

So, what distinguished higher performers from lower performers? Higher performers exhibit the following characteristics:

- **Execute Strategies Better.** That is, companies that enjoy higher performance (based on the aforementioned four factors) also tend to be better at executing strategies (based on two different survey indicators).

- **Provide Clarity.** Out of the top six major areas of difference between higher and lower performers, three of them (clear strategy, clear goals, and clear focus) deal with clarity. *"Creating a clear strategy"* was ranked as the single most important action for companies implementing strategies. What's more, out of 57 different approaches to strategy execution, *"defining clear goals to support strategy"* was ranked second in importance, (*"ensuring clear accountability"* was fourth, and *"having a clear focus on implementing/ executing strategy"* was sixth). Clarity facilitates and enables organizational alignment.

- **Utilize Alignment Strategies.** Specifically, higher performers are more likely to tie organizational objectives to strategy and to analyze and subsequently align processes, people and tools to enable their successful completion.

- **Exhibit Superior Speed and Adaptability.** The practice revealing the largest difference between higher and lower performers is *"demonstrating the ability to quickly and effectively execute when new strategic opportunities arise."* Another strategic action showing a distinct separation between companies is *"having an adaptive organizational infrastructure"*. These two items suggest that adaptive organizational infrastructures – in combination with an emphasis on clarity – help organizations react more quickly to new strategic opportunities.

In summary, devising strategies is more than a linear exercise. It requires an understanding of the organization's current capabilities given its existing people/culture, workflow processes, and tools/ systems. Once both the potential and the limits of the organization are identified, then a realistic direction and set of goals can be established, and a clear vision for the company and its particular promise to the marketplace emerges. Strategy Activation then defines that vision and aligns the organization's internal mechanisms to most effectively achieve it.

KEEPING PROMISES: QWEST COMMUNICATIONS

Smart companies also need to know how to make wine out of vinegar. That is, they not only need to practice flexibility in devising new strategies, but also work within their given circumstances. Richard Notebaert realized that his company urgently needed a shift in policy and a brand new strategy when he took the reins as CEO of Qwest Communications. He discovered that over a period of eight years (from 1994 through 2002) Qwest's customer satisfaction ratings plunged 27 percent. Qwest needed to build a strategy that would reverse how it was increasingly being perceived in the marketplace.

In the past, Qwest approached the marketplace as a technology leader leveraging its DSL advantage. While Qwest concentrated on the strategy of delivering superior technology, its customer satisfaction ratings plummeted. Ultimately, the Colorado state attorney general sued Qwest for violating that state's consumer protection law, alleging fraudulent billing practices, high-pressure sales tactics, and improper issue resolution procedures. It was time for a change.

Qwest launched a new customer-centric strategy in October 2002. Replacing its old strategy of technology leadership (encapsulated by *"Ride the Light"*) with a new strategy – world-class customer service (described as the *"Spirit of Service"*) – Qwest changed its logo and launched an aggressive ad campaign. Qwest's employees spoke directly to the viewer, promising change and emphasizing the organization's renewed commitment to its customers.

A sampling of the messages the company conveyed are listed below:

- *"Watch us now"*
- *"Now we're going to change Telecommunications for the better."*
- *"It's the right thing for the customers."*
- *"[We're] putting the customer first."*
- *"This is the spirit of service."*

Qwest did a fabulous job communicating its new strategy to the market and showing clear intent. It made a promise to change and put the customer first.

In order for Qwest to keep its promise, the company would have to translate its marketing pledge into new employee responsibilities and actions. This process is exactly what Strategy Activation enables organizations to accomplish.

Let's contemplate the role of a Qwest CSR (Customer Service Representative), who must now provide the new *"Spirit of Service"* when answering customer calls. First of all, what does that term specifically mean? How does one define good service? Defining and aligning strategic goals within the context of every-day work is essential. It means that every CSR must understand what types of behavior will be expected (and rewarded).

As illustrated in Figure 1.1 below, CSR Mary thinks good service involves personally resolving an issue in real time no matter how long the call takes. CSR Stan decides that good service means helping as many customers each day as possible. Finally, there's CSR Janet who feels that good service means saving her customers money on their bills.

Figure 1.1—Hypothetical Interpretations of the Spirit of Service

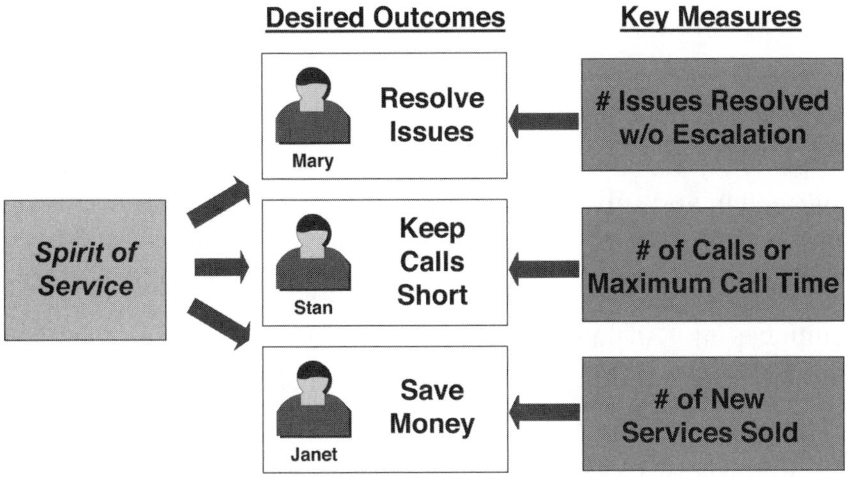

Each of these CSRs makes a legitimate interpretation of putting the customer first – *"the Spirit of Service"*. In this hypothetical example, the customer experience would vary dramatically from one CSR to the next. If customer Mike gets CSR Mary, she could keep him on the phone forever, but if he gets CSR Stan, Stan might rush through a resolution without really addressing the problem. CSR Janet may try to sell Mike new products that can save him money without even considering the issue he originally phoned in about.

To create a consistent, unified implementation, an organization must convert the strategy – in this case, *"Spirit of Service"* – into clear roles and responsibilities for each individual, defining what he or she must do on a daily basis to support and implement that strategy.

How performance is measured and rewarded (whether on issue resolutions, call time, or services sold) will determine how CSRs behave with customers. Of course, it is human nature to look to maximize rewards. Accordingly, the measurement and reward systems must tie directly back to the employee behaviors the organization wishes to encourage.

Many companies fail to relate business strategies to the realities of their daily business practices. By ignoring the details, they often end up moving too fast into areas they cannot hope to succeed in and subsequently break the promise communicated to their customers. Strategy Activation helps companies avoid this dangerous pitfall. By looking closely at each strategy *before* it launches and making the appropriate adjustments required to align people, workflow processes, and tools/systems, companies have a much better chance of keeping every promise they make. My promise to you is that, in *Chapter 2,* we'll begin to show you how Strategy Activation makes that happen.

CHAPTER TWO

MAKING PROMISES

*"Any intelligent fool can make things bigger and
more complex...It takes a touch of genius—and a lot of courage
to move in the opposite direction."*
—Albert Einstein

"Vision+Execution= Success"
—Anon

WHAT MAKES A GOOD STRATEGY?

Here's a common story, and a sad one at that. Emboldened by the enthusiasm of a successful annual retreat, upper management approves a technically brilliant and theoretically sound strategy. Yet by the next annual retreat, loyal customers are confused, front line employees find the new strategy irrelevant (or worse yet they haven't even heard of the strategy!), and market share has not changed for the better. The once "brilliant" strategy is relegated to the failure bin.

What happened?

The problem with many business strategies is that they are often written to showcase the talents (rather than long-term vision and realism) of the strategist, and often remain unconnected to the existing infrastructure and true capabilities of the corporation. The result? Strategies become highly impractical in execution.

The best strategies are usually the simplest. Simple strategies are easy to communicate to a number of players, especially in a company with many kinds of employees on multiple corporate tiers. Simple strategies inspire clear, powerful marketing campaigns. Most importantly, if a strategy is easy to communicate and easy to comprehend, then the essential alignment of policies and procedures and "go-to-market" plans around that strategy will be straightforward. Simplicity also allows for another important asset given the current rate of technological change: flexibility.

Simple, however, does not mean easy. Forming good strategies means translating all of the complicated needs and buying trends of your current (and future) customer base into your company's market advantage. Add a healthy dose of realism to that equation and the process of forming a strategy starts looking more like a continual process rather than an isolated brainstorming exercise.

The type of strategy I refer to goes by many names, including brand strategy, unique selling proposition, go-to-market strategy, value proposition, and market positioning, but in the end they all boil down to the same thing: a marketplace promise. While legions of authors and consultants will have us believe that each of the "strategy types" listed above brings a unique and necessary nuance to your business plan, it's ultimately the promise that's important. Whether you promise to provide top quality products, superior customer service or the lowest prices, you are making a pledge in the marketplace, and you will have to align all the other aspects of your business to keep it.

Strategy Activation is appropriate when a strategy creates a distinct expectation in the minds of the customers. Operating strategies, such as capital financing, human resource management, or raw material procurement, do not tend to elicit a consumer expectation. Strategy Activation links a company's goals back to its customers' wants and needs. Meeting customers' expectations requires the holistic, company-wide approach to strategy implementation that Strategy Activation facilitates.

Let me give you an example: consumers now expect that Wal-Mart will always have the low price. That's Wal-Mart's marketplace promise. It's how they both define themselves and distinguish themselves from their competition.

In order to execute its low price strategy, Wal-Mart needed to create an entire infrastructure (people, processes, and tools) that delivered low prices while still making a profit. A well-though-out raw material and/or finished goods procurement strategy remains essential to delivering low prices. Yet the customer doesn't know or care about procurement strategy. All the customer wants is low prices.

So, while operating processes (e.g. procurement, order fulfillment) are integral to serving the customer, they don't themselves create a marketplace promise. However, they are crucial to *delivery* on that promise and are thus a direct outgrowth of Strategy Activation.

WHERE DISCONNECTS ORIGINATE

Many strategies start as a blank sheet of paper. The company surveys the marketplace to determine what customers want, what the competition is promising and the relevant gaps between the two. Rarely is consideration given to the existing condition of the organization.

In short, disconnect begins to occur when companies make a marketplace promise without first completing a self-assessment of their own competencies. When this situation occurs, it is because companies often make one or both of the following common mistakes early in their strategy formulation process:

1) Not recognizing the current capabilities and limitations of the organization.

    Or

2) Overestimating how much change the organization can absorb in pursuit of the strategy.

Either misstep can have a tremendous negative impact when it comes time to deliver on the promise. Well-designed plans are important, but they must always be coupled with a clear understanding of the required resulting actions.

Remember, a good strategy brilliantly executed will always trump a brilliant strategy poorly executed.

Think of Strategy Activation as the link between your company's stated objectives on paper and your achieved goals in the bank. To succeed as a company in an increasingly knowledge-based economy, you have to think well beyond your current market position. Where are the real (and future) market gaps and needs in your industry? But as you aim high, keep your objectives grounded. Do you have the right organizational capabilities and capacity? Have you established a realistic timeline? Is there a clear chain of responsibility? Can you remain flexible and responsive to consumers' many demands? What obstacles do you anticipate and how do you plan to overcome them?

Take it from Bill Gates and Wal-Mart.

Bill Gates, founder of Microsoft, understood the strategic importance of identifying his company's strengths and outwitting his competitors in the marketplace. In Gates's early strategy he wisely avoided wasting time in areas where other competitors were already strong and focused instead on superseding them at their weak points. By entering a rapidly growing market without too many competitors early on, Gates established Microsoft as an industry leader. When Microsoft then committed itself to continually raising the industry bar and adding more innovative products to its line, customers started to *expect and buy* new products and technology from the company.

Aggressive strategies can also be launched simply to wound the competition, exemplified by the type of damage Wal-Mart generates in what is now termed the "Wal-Mart effect." When the same flat panel TVs that were supplying many electronics companies with healthy profit margins became deeply discounted at Wal-Mart, it sent stores like Circuit City reeling. Slashing screen prices created a high visibility, loss leader at Wal-Mart, where sales of high definition TVs formed a small percentage of the chain's overall sales. Other major electronic stores such as Tweeter, where flat panel TVs constituted more than half of overall sales, were left with major losses and layoffs.

CRITERIA FOR CHOOSING A VIABLE STRATEGY

There are three general rules of thumb when it comes to settling on a strategy:

1) Your strategy must leverage the existing capabilities of your company. It must also continually anticipate, innovate, and stretch your company's strengths in an ever-changing marketplace.

2) Your strategy must communicate a compelling and relevant promise to customers. Whether it's swifter turnaround time or lower prices, the promise must be responsive to a true market need to gain any traction.

3) Your strategy must be devised so that it distinguishes your company and your business from the competition.

"People should stop focusing on the sexy stuff and instead should focus on the nuts and bolts," advised Dan Coughlin, long-time strategy consultant and president of The Coughlin Co. in Fenton, Missouri, referring to the failure of DreamWorks to achieve their long-term goals in the film industry.

In other words, while DreamWorks sought to differentiate itself by building a business based on creative autonomy, which sounds great on paper; in the end it didn't produce enough movies and box office hits to achieve financial success.

A strategy in and of itself will never be enough. The key lies in executing it flawlessly. That means capitalizing on your existing strengths. You can only truly and consistently deliver those products and services that your organization's people, processes, and tools/systems are capable of generating. Anything else is just empty talk.

Allow me to offer a personal account to demonstrate the point. For many, many years I was a loyal Circuit City customer. They were my go-to retailer for stereo equipment, TVs, VCRs, DVD players, and computers. The products were reasonably priced and the salespeople were adequately attentive and informed.

About three years ago my wife needed a new PDA. While I was inclined to make the purchase online, she felt the need to touch and feel the product before buying. So we trundled off to Circuit City. As we entered the store, we were greeted by a huge new banner that proclaimed (and I paraphrase), *"We promise you the best customer experience possible."* While I wasn't exactly sure how the company defined *"best customer experience,"* this seemed like a great strategy. I prepared myself to be wowed by what I assumed was a new commitment to service.

We walked over to the PDA display. A salesperson was working diligently to connect a new PDA that had just arrived. We waited a moment. When it became clear his task would take some time, we asked him if he carried Model *XYZ*. Without even glancing our way, he simply said "*yes*" and continued with his task. We asked if we could see the product. He said, "*Sure, when I'm finished doing this.*"

This was not my definition of a satisfying customer experience. The promise remained unfulfilled. We left the store and I haven't been back since. Why? Because on that day we rediscovered Best Buy.

BEST BUY: THE CHALLENGES OF STRATEGY EXECUTION

Once upon a time, Best Buy, the leading electronics retailer, was far better known for low prices (hence the name) and scarce staffing than for friendly, knowledgeable employees who could answer detailed questions. This strategy served the company well as it rapidly expanded in a time when consumers craved affordable TVs, stereos, and refrigerators. Then the influx of more complex electronic toys shifted the needs of the market-place. The computer became a mainstream household appliance. Feature laden cell phones and digital cameras vied for attention. People stopped buying TVs and stereos and started buying home theaters.

The suddenly vast selection of electronic options made choosing the right product much more difficult for the average consumer. In fact, the very notion of the "average consumer" no longer applied. Customers ran the gamut from the very knowledgeable to the deeply uninformed. While everyone knew how to turn on a TV and change the channel, few could navigate the intricacies of a home theater system. To meet the needs of this new marketplace reality, Best Buy needed a change in strategy.

The chain unleashed a bold new campaign of "*Customer-Centricity*" – increasing staff and revamping training for salespeople, along with identifying and ordering inventory for many stores around several different "market segments" they themselves identified. The company recognized that the customers' needs varied considerably from the tech-savvy to the neophytes, and it responded by tailoring the customer experience to each market segment. Meanwhile, its chief competitor, Circuit City, continued to treat each customer in the same manner and watched its market share steadily decline as a result.

Brad Anderson, CEO of Best Buy, strove to differentiate the brand through the customer's improved shopping experience, rolling out the new policy in 300 of Best Buy's 741 stores. Addressing the change, Anderson stated that:

> *"The first thing we did to differentiate ourselves was taken directly from discount-store chains. ...In our world the way you win the game isn't the price of the TV – which is about the same for all retailers – but the experience you give customers once they are in our stores."*

Implementation of the customer-centric strategic vision required a new level of expertise and sophistication on the sales floor. To provide the right individualized customer experience Best Buy's salespeople must:

- Instantly identify which segment a consumer matches and alter their selling approach to that which is most effective for that segment.
- Determine what the consumer's specific needs are through a series of discovery questions.

- Recommend a product solution that meets those needs.

It is difficult, however, for one person to be an expert on the needs of every segment, and Best Buy had to add staff to implement the strategy. Separate managers were hired to concentrate on each segment. As a result some stores had a general manager and as many as five assistant managers. In the redesigned stores Best Buy employed an average of 120 full and part-time employees per store. Circuit City, by comparison, had 60 workers per store.

The company's competitive shift in policy demonstrated that Best Buy chose to listen and respond to its customers. By investing more (primarily by increasing staff levels in conjunction with training requirements) and allowing local stores more autonomy, the company looked to differentiate itself in the marketplace. In many ways they succeeded.

Best Buy's earnings went up 20 percent, surpassing its own internal sales goals! Much of this growth could be directly traced to the new strategic approach and customer focused policies. CEO Anderson commented on these results:

"Our customer-centric business model gives us the confidence to be able to grow outside of the United States. We know that we must do three seemingly simple things to succeed: gain deep insights into our customers' priorities and lifestyles; figure out how we can encourage and nurture employee ingenuity on behalf of our customers; and then offer solutions that will result in great experiences for our customers,"

Yet, for all its strengths, Best Buy's strategy still might have an Achilles heel. While improved staff morale and innovative customer service struck a chord in the marketplace, Best Buy might not have adequately examined the increased costs in infrastructure to determine if the strategy could be sustained in the long-term. The transformations it sought required a major investment in operations, both in time and money. In December, 2005 the company disclosed that its sales and administrative expenses rose 22 percent in the third quarter – more than double the company's overall sales increase. The news caused Best Buy's stock to fall 12 percent in a single day. Analysts loved the customer-centric strategy but couldn't swallow the increased operating expenses. Some worried that ultimately the company might not be able to keep up the investments necessary to continue to meet the standards its new promise had set in motion.

The lesson of the story is that the complexities of implementing strategies are not always seen up front and can lead to problems down the road. In other words, promises are often hard to keep (and keep up with) in the long run.

In response to Wall Street's disappointment, CEO Brad Anderson issued a statement in early 2006 that the company must *"trim some fat."* This announcement coupled with a number of layoffs left a big question mark in the marketplace. Will Best Buy be able to keep up with its own strategy? Will staff morale suffer? Will the company keep its promise over time?

STICK TO YOUR STRENGTHS – A MODERN BUSINESS PARABLE

It is important to keep your strategies aligned with your strengths and not lose focus by chasing after spurious targets like the latest technological trends. I once worked with a leading mortgage lender who often did business through independent third party mortgage brokers. Lenders compete to capture the lion's share of any individual broker's business. As you would expect, successful lenders have built their business around their historical strengths. They differentiate themselves from competitors through price, service, technology, product innovations, etc. Some are recognized as product innovators, some as low price leaders, still others as technology leaders and so on.

My client was recognized for superior high touch service. Theirs was a face-to-face business. When you called the office, a real person answered. When you encountered a problem, an account executive came for a personal visit. This strategy served the client as a well-executed key point of differentiation from the competition. Eventually, external factors changed the competitive landscape. The extended refinance boom of the first half of this decade (driven by historically low interest rates) put a significant capacity strain on the mortgage industry. There were just too many loans and not enough lenders to process them. Service levels started to fall across the board. While lenders rushed to add capacity, they couldn't respond fast enough and as a result closings moved out farther and farther.

Some lenders responded by adding more technology to their infrastructure. Voice recognition units replaced real people answering the phones; online portals replaced face-to-face visits to brokers' offices. Much of this new technology resulted in quick, short-term share gains for some lenders because it created increased processing capacity at a crucial time. My client, seeing this drive toward technology, immediately made plans to invest huge sums of money in the new technologies. Consequently these tools removed the one-on-one contact that historically distinguished them in the marketplace. Yet the client believed that because the technology leaders were gaining share, this is what the marketplace wanted.

This assumption proved to be untrue. The technology leaders were gaining share because they had the additional capacity in an extreme situation, not because the market hungered for a low touch environment. As we all know, the mortgage industry is cyclical. Eventually the pressure for capacity was going to ebb.

Not recognizing the true economic and business factors, my client chose to chase the technology leaders. Now remember, technology development wasn't their historical strength. They abandoned their original strategy of high touch service (which afforded them positioning, image, promise and differentiation) for a strategy in which they had never previously demonstrated a strong competency. They cut back investments in recruiting and training of personnel and instead pursued new advanced systems.

At the client's request, I went into the marketplace and interviewed a broad spectrum of their customers. The results were quite educational. Brokers bemoaned the loss of my client's personalized service orientation. The brokers felt that my client would be unable to match the advances of the technology leaders and would no longer stand out without the high touch service element they had previously fostered. It appeared my client risked losing their relevancy and with it preferred vendor status with many of their loyal customers.

By abandoning a core competency (personalized service) and pursuing a new strategy (technology leadership), my client disregarded their best marketplace strategy. Both personalized service and technology leadership are viable strategies. The question that needed to be answered was which strategy was viable for my client? Which promise was most easily made and kept?

CHAPTER THREE

MAKING PROMISES CREDIBLE

"In the 1960s, if you introduced a new product to America, 90% of the people who viewed it for the first time believed in the corporate promise. Then 40 years later if you performed the same exercise less than 10% of the public believed it was true. The fracturing of trust is based on the fact that the consumer has been let down."
—Howard Schultz

Yes, I made so many promises that never did come true But sweetheart, no matter what else I ever do You are my Forever Love and this is my last promise to you Until the end of time ... I'll be in love with you!
—Joanne Murray Vereb from *Broken Promises*

The thing about promises and love is that people love to break promises.

Don't believe me? Well, neither did I until I conducted a quick, informal experiment.

Recently, I Googled the term "making promises." The search drew 259,000 hits. Then I Googled "keeping promises." That query garnered 148,000 hits. Lastly, I Googled "broken promises."

I hit the motherload! The term "broken promises" drew a whopping 1,210,000 hits – far more than the other two search terms combined.

Okay, while my little study's bonafides aren't exactly up to Harvard Business School standards, the experiment does seem to show that we have a lot more to say about breaking promises than making or keeping them.

Maybe that's because breaking promises is no longer an anomaly in our culture. In fact, maybe breaking promises *defines* our culture. Most of the themes linked to my Google searches were from the political world, where Republicans and Democrats both absorbed blows from enraged constituents. And it's not like the U.S. has a monopoly on broken political promises. According to the press reports, the UN has not kept the promises of its founding, the British and Canadian Prime Ministers have failed their countries, the Israelis and Palestinians have broken promises to each other, and the Western democracies have broken their promises to the African continent.

Of course, the business world is also rife with broken promises. Scores of companies have broken pension promises to retirees, management has broken promises to labor, corrupt CEOs have broken trust with shareholders, and products often fail to live up to their hype. Where does it end?

I'll get to that question in a moment, but let's first discuss the impact of diminished – or disappointed – expectations. With the multitude of broken promises weighing down on society, is anyone surprised that consumers are skeptical of promises? We learn at an early age that companies will make practically impossible claims to attract our business. Kites that didn't fly, disappointingly two-dimensional "3-D" glasses and Sea Monkeys that looked absolutely nothing like monkeys, if you could see them at all, are but a few examples of the realities of some pretty wild promises. Maybe that was our culture's "A-Ha!" moment, when we finally received that first toy we saw on Saturday morning TV and realized it wasn't nearly as cool as it looked in the commercial. In other words, we got our first taste of unmet expectations. When our fast food burger looked nothing like it did on the menu we learned that food products don't always taste as good as they look. And when our first pair of P.F. Flyer sneakers didn't really help us "run faster and jump higher," we started to get the gist of "over promise, under deliver."

BREAKING THE "MARKETPLACE PROMISE"

So it goes with "marketplace promises." A marketplace (or brand) promise is no different from what we've been discussing in chapters one and two. Simply defined, a marketplace promise is:

- What the business – your business – promises to deliver to the customer.
- Your image, defining what you stand for in the marketplace.
- How you distinguish yourself from competition.

A while back, the magazine *BrandWeek* offered a very revealing article on broken promises that examined the gap between what customers want and what customers get.

In the article reporter Jim Edwards chronicles the saga of a nine-year-old San Francisco girl who had an idea to improve Apple's popular iPod Nano product. She thought the company should include visual song lyrics in the device so people could sing along to their favorite tunes – a pretty good idea.

The little girl wrote a letter to Apple CEO Steve Jobs explaining her idea and asked for a response. She got one, just not the response she was expecting. After 90 days or so the girl received a form letter from Apple's legal department stating the company does not accept unsolicited ideas and directed her to the company's legal section of Apple's corporate web site. There, she would presumably read up on what fate awaits her if she burdened Apple and Mr. Jobs any further.

Upon reading the missive from Apple, the girl, according to her mother, "went to her room and slammed the door. She was very upset."

Okay, ticking off competitors like Bill Gates is one thing. Making a despondent nine-year-old girl slam her bedroom door is quite another. CBS News soon acquired the letter and went national with it on its evening news broadcast. After CBS aired the piece, bloggers took up the cause, issuing online boycott demands against Apple and accusing it of "making little girls cry."

Apple's ham-fisted response to one of its customers is "Exhibit A" in how to do as much damage to your image as possible. As Edwards put it, "The fact that a nine-year-old girl thinks Jobs might be interested in her suggestions indicates that Apple's brand is strong – strong enough that even very young consumers feel they have a relationship with the company.

"The fact that Jobs has a lousy system for dealing with well-intentioned letters (let alone ones from kids) indicates something else: Even the best [companies] can fail to deliver on the expectations of their most loyal patrons."

A NATIONAL TREND

As the article suggests, Apple isn't the only company tarnishing its own image by disappointing customers. A 2006 customer expectations study by the New York City marketing firm Brand Keys shows that the average level of customer expectations (as measured by their Loyalty Index) across 35 product categories rose 4.5% from one year earlier. Apparently, companies aren't up to the task. The numbers show that, over the same period, the average ability of brands to meet those expectations declined by 9.2%. Said another way, customer expectations are rising faster than companies' ability to satisfy them. That disparity is not a one-time anomaly, either. According to Brand Keys president Robert Passikoff, the gap is expanding every year. "Expectations have increased in all categories," he told Brand Week. "It's an ongoing pattern."

Sure, customers can be demanding, and we often condition them to be more demanding. Once you bump up a car rental driver to a Cadillac or upgrade a traveler to a luxury hotel suite, you reset the bar for that customer's expectations. The customer is disappointed when the next experience doesn't include a similar upgrade. It's almost ironic that companies' desire to exceed customer expectations often only heightens those expectations, which leads to lower overall customer satisfaction. For a lot of products, the bar is now set impossibly high. Consider the bottled water industry. Water is water. As the *BrandWeek* article points out, bottled water products are barely indistinguishable from one another. Even though most customers would agree with that assertion, consumer expectations for bottled water still grew 8% from 2005 to 2006. What more were they expecting?

"Imagine the Dasani or Aquafina brand steward responsible for meeting those expectations," writes *BrandWeek*. "What do you do? Triple filter? Reverse osmosis? Vitamins? Flavors? It's all been done. Now what? How do you make water 8% more refreshing? Then do it again next year. And the year after that. At some point, water will be 100% refreshing (if it isn't already) and then what?"

Perhaps a company like Southwest is the blueprint for success. The airline, famous for its "we're just plain folks running a simple airline" mantra, has set customer expectations so low that they are consistently viewed by the public as a company that surpasses expectations. Compared to most other airlines, which go to great lengths to promise passengers a comfortable, almost luxurious ride only to fail to deliver one, Southwest's simple style plays well in Peoria and beyond. Under promise and over deliver!

OFTEN, PROMISES AREN'T ENOUGH

I'm with Abraham Lincoln, who once said, "We must not promise what we ought not, lest we be called on to perform what we cannot."

Your customers understand what Honest Abe was saying. In fact, the current generation of customers and consumers has heard it all and now believes very little. They are a skeptical bunch, and with good reason. We've been disappointed by one broken promise after another all of our lives. As a result, customers know to take everything companies tell them with a grain of salt.

My colleague, Alan Bergstrom, speaks of "permissions and limits" – boundaries placed on an organization by the marketplace. Customers maintain preconceived notions about an organization's capabilities based largely on experience and the organization's image in the marketplace. These boundaries define the outer limits of the organization's credibility. For example, few would believe that McDonalds could serve up a delicious, finely aged sirloin steak cooked to perfection. Given what we know today of McDonald's we just can't believe that promise.

So simply making a promise isn't enough to get people to flock to your door. You have to give them a credible promise AND a reason to believe that your promise isn't just one of the many empty promises they hear everyday.

For example:

- You promise me speed? Why should I believe you can deliver speed?
- You promise me luxury? How are you going to deliver luxury?

- You promise me safety and security? Can you really keep me safe?

The promise is WHAT you say you're going to do. The reason to believe the promise comes from your explanation of HOW you're going to do it.

- I'm going to deliver speed by flying your packages overnight to your destination rather than truck them (Fed Ex)
- I'm going to deliver luxury by giving you the Heavenly Bed (Westin Hotels)
- You will be safeguarded by our Roll Over Protection System (Volvo XC90)

Like many in marketing today, we call these the pillars of the promise. They are the "how" of the "what." They give a customer the detail he or she needs to make an informed decision. Not only are the customers evaluating the promise itself, but they also get to evaluate how the promise will be fulfilled. Both must be credible, of course. As we pointed out above, you wouldn't believe that McDonalds could put a juicy steak on your tray (a promise) no matter how many "hows" they give you. Sorry…they just can't make me believe that promise unless they come clean and admit they'll buy the steak at the restaurant next door. Nor would you believe that Hilton Hotels could provide a new level of luxury (certainly a believable promise) by putting more towels in the room. How would providing more under-sized towels make my experience more luxurious? So the lesson here is that we must start with a promise that can be believed and support it with pillars that enhance that credibility.

MARRIOT HOTELS: A BETTER NIGHT'S STAY

According to its website, Marriott Hotels & Resorts, the flagship brand of Marriott International, commands first choice preference among business travelers, leisure travelers, and meeting planners. They also claim the highest customer preference of any lodging brand in the United States. With over 500 full-service, upscale hotels Marriott Hotels & Resorts surround their guests with services and amenities that inspire them to perform at their peak while enjoying memorable experiences.

Marriott Hotels & Resorts focuses on the "Achievement Guest," which they define as individuals who are driven to perform and who thrive on excellence. This need to achieve may be driven by a desire to please their company or their family or may simply be borne of their own need for a sense of accomplishment.

Marriott's promise to this Achievement Guest is elegant in its simplicity:

PROMISE: INSPIRING PERFORMANCE

In essence they are promising to inspire a guest's performance, thereby meeting that guest's need to achieve. This marketplace promise is supported and fulfilled by three pillars. They provide the driving force behind the chosen services, features, and amenities Marriott provides to inspire the Achievement Guest.

PILLARS:

Achieve

The professional, performance-driven side of Marriott's guests and hotels. Examples include large, well-lit, ergonomic work desks that pivot to enable the guest to create an environment conducive to work in his or her room.

Revive

Purposeful luxury and more personal elements of the guest's stay, such as aromatherapy bath products, 300-thread-count sheets, and connectivity panels on a high-definition TV that enable guests to connect personal entertainment devices such as iPods.

Culture

Warm, friendly, sincere service built on the company's Spirit to Serve® business pledge to provide a refreshingly human touch in today's hectic world.

THE NEW GUEST ROOM

How does Marriott use its pillars to drive implementation in the marketplace? The answer is not so complicated. The pillars help Marriott stay focused on the promise it's made and the defining activities it believes will meet the Achievement Guest's needs and expectations.

The artwork in the rooms reflects the local environment. The spacious rooms include the hotel's signature bed from Marriott, including full-sized headboards, quilted top mattresses, upgraded down blankets, oversized down comforters, 300-thread-count linens, and down and feather pillows – amenities that help the Achievement Guest **revive** to perform at his or her peak the next day.

Some of Marriott's hotels will offer a flat panel, high-definition television that serves as more than just a television – it's also a monitor for laptops, and the built-in, split screen capability allows guests to work and watch their favorite program at the same time. Well-lit desks with ample workspace, task lighting, ergonomic seating, high-speed Internet access, and connectivity panels for iPods, Blackberries, and other personal entertainment devices further enable guests to **achieve** their business goals.

PERFORMANCE

An unwavering commitment to its own marketplace promise and supporting pillars has moved Marriott into an enviable competitive position. A number of 2004/2005 tracking surveys placed Marriott at the top of the list for consumer preference among lodging brands in the United States. In 2006 Marriott Hotels & Resorts achieved a RevPAR (revenue per available room) index of 112.3%, reflecting a market share premium. That same year Marriott was rated "Best Hotel Chain" for business travel by both *Business Traveler* and *Executive Travel*.

As Marriott continues to expand it will also continue to focus on its marketplace promise of Inspiring Performance in an ongoing effort to win over Achievement Guests. By combining the experiential elements of the pillars with the company's foundational commitment to operational excellence, Marriott hopes to solidify and lengthen its leading position in the marketplace.

DUNLOP TIRES: A FITTING SET OF WHEELS

It's obviously not just Marriott; plenty of other companies have recognized the need to create a compelling brand promise supported by convincing evidence. Like Marriott, Dunlop Tires' website has given us some detailed insight into their brand promise (circa 2004) and how they chose to fulfill that promise in the marketplace.

So what did Dunlop Tires promise its customers? **Performance!** Pure and simple. As Dunlop summarized it, "The smell of hot rubber and the crunch of asphalt beneath beefy wheels are two of life's finest experiences. Dunlop is about driving. Driving is about Dunlop."

The company listed five reasons (or pillars) why consumers should believe Dunlop's promise of performance:

1) Innovative new products
2) Linkage to the world's most prestigious auto brands
3) European Heritage

4) Linkage to the racing circuits

5) Cutting edge website

Reason #1: In short, it's all about new products. An initiative, launched in 2004, cites the Dunlop SP Sport Maxx flagship for the brand's ultra performance tire lineup, the Direzza DZ101 for the fast-growing vehicle tuner segment and the Dunlop Grandtrek AT20 highway light truck tire for luxury and crossover sport utility vehicles as new products that can "revitalize the brand," making "innovative new products" the first of "Dunlop's Five Reasons to Believe." "New products are the lifeblood of our business," said Andy Traicoff, director of Dunlop consumer tire marketing.

Reasons #2: The second "Reason to Believe" – leveraging prestigious original equipment fitments – stems from the brand's visibility on the world's finest automobiles. With original equipment tire fitments on Audi, BMW, Range Rover, Lexus, Mazda, Mitsubishi, Porsche, Toyota, and Volkswagen, Dunlop "has cemented its reputation among luxury and performance car owners, light truck and sport utility vehicle owners – and those who aspire to be owners of those brands," Traicoff said. The director added that premium luxury brands typically score higher in customer satisfaction surveys, and consumers are far more likely to seek the same tire brand at replacement time. "Prestigious fitment on these vehicles also makes it easier for salespersons behind the counter to sell Dunlop replacement tires. They can point to a company, such as BMW, and give customers a reason to believe in the tire. Prestige goes a long way in ensuring our success in the marketplace," he added.

Reason #3: Leveraging Dunlop's European/racing heritage was the third "Reason to Believe." Benefiting from its reputation as a performance leader in the fields of European automobiles and racing, Dunlop tries to play to its customers' emotional connection with their cars, Traicoff said. "It's a tribute to a time when racing was a gentleman's sport and road races were held on some of the most breathtaking streets of Europe. It's about the romanticism of driving, the thrill of competition and the importance of heritage and performance. It's an emotion that continues today among enthusiasts who personalize their vehicles and those who enjoy showing their cars at Concours d'Elegance or Hot Import Nights events," he said. Thanks to the rapid retail growth in the past six years of performance products used to modify sport compact cars, Dunlop stands ready to gain share and sales. These automotive enthusiasts account for 22.5 million replacement tire sales annually, Traicoff said.

Reason #4: Broad commitment to and participation in the sport of racing was the fourth "Reason to Believe." To boost its performance image, Dunlop sponsors Formula D Drifting, NHRA Summit Import drag racing series and NDRA "NOPI Drag Wars" Race Series. The brand also produces sport compact race slicks for professional drag racers and a track-event tire called the SP Supersport Race. Dunlop has a strong reputation in auto and motorcycle racing circuits in the United States, Europe, Australia and Japan. "We're always looking for co-marketing events in North America that make sense for the Dunlop brand. The main criteria is that they reach 'In-the-Know' enthusiasts," Traicoff said.

Reason #5: The fifth "Reason to Believe" was the dunloptires.com website that dared to be different. The site continues to reinvent itself to cater to automotive enthusiasts and their lifestyles. Traicoff said the website is used to build tire sales at local retailers.

We learn at a very young age that it's bad form to make promises you can't keep. Why this message hasn't translated well to the business world is perplexing.

The only certainty in today's marketplace is that if you make a promise and don't deliver, your customers will go off and find someone who can.

After all, we live in the information age, when data and awareness about your competitors is only a click away. As customer expectations increase, the cost of over promising and under delivering has never been so high.

CONCLUSION

Not all promises are created equal. While there are many viable paths to choose from, each organization carries its unique marketplace permissions and organizational competencies. Your BEST marketplace promise depends on several important factors:

- Is your marketplace promise compelling to your customers and will it distinguish you from your competitors? What do customers want from their provider? What needs are not being adequately provided by others?
- What permissions and limits have customers placed on you? The marketplace has to believe in your ability to keep the promise.
- Do you have credible reasons for the customer to believe your promise? What assurances can you provide that your promise will be delivered in the marketplace?
- Can you consistently deliver on the promise? What current or new capabilities support marketplace implementation?

Finding the right promise that resonates best with your target customer is the critical first step. But making empty promises is a futile and unprofitable exercise. So let's move on to the next chapter and start exploring how to keep the marketplace promises we make.

CHAPTER FOUR

KEEPING PROMISES

*"Don't ever promise more than you can deliver, but always
deliver more than you promise."*
—Lou Holtz

*"There is only one boss. The customer. And he or she can fire
everybody in the company from the chairman on down,
simply by spending his or her money somewhere else."*
—Sam Walton

Anyone who walks into a Wal-Mart can tell that giving
Wal-Mart customers what they want – value – is a big priority.
But understanding your customers' needs are one thing,
fulfilling them is an entirely different proposition. Strategies can
and do fail routinely—simply because implementation is problematic.
Many strategies focus almost exclusively on market properties,
primarily defining what business to be in. However, knowing what
market to pursue and gleaning the intimate details of its
constituents is not a unique talent. Over the past few decades,
the routine use of statistical analysis, data mining, focus groups,
the internet, and market research consultants has eliminated the
guesswork used in determining what customers want. In fact,
market strategy has had so much attention and resources devoted
to it that it could almost be considered a commodity in a growing
number of industries. The choice of market segment and manner
of approaching a defined demographic is no longer a sustainable
competitive advantage.

Keeping promises made to the customer is the new paradigm for success. Promises that are made about a product or service and how its experience will completely delight the consumer. But keeping promises is a highly developed skill. It requires the organization making them to effectively execute on a continuous basis.

Strategy development, therefore, cannot be isolated and conducted separate from its execution. It must consider and align with the implementation side of the business operations. Implementation touches the customer – and businesses are defined by their customers' experiences. The differences in mindsets between strategy and execution are significant. Take a look at table 4.1 to view some of the major characteristics of strategy as opposed to implementation.

Table 4.1—Strategy versus Implementation

STRATEGY (Includes)	IMPLEMENTATION (Includes)
• Performing Market Analysis • Conducting Market Research • Developing Theories • Planning for Alternatives • Making the Promise to the Customer	• Acquiring and Cultivating Customers • Delivering Products & Services • Resolving Customer Issues • Managing Touchpoints • Keeping the Promise to the Customer

Think of having a well-defined strategy as a key foundation for a business. You've ambitiously started something, but the foundation must be aligned with the business to be built above it, and vice versa.

EXAMPLES OF COMPANIES EXECUTING THEIR STRATEGY

Fortunately for our purposes there exist a number of fine companies that can see the whole picture. Let's take a look at and then explore the following examples set forth by the companies below:

- McDonalds restaurant maintains a strategy that delivers meals cheaply, quickly, and in a consistent manner from its numerous convenient locations.
- Apple delivers computers and multimedia technology products that are design-oriented, user friendly, and targeted to the creative person.
- Barnes and Noble Booksellers maintains a successful physical storefront presence for the retail sale of books and music despite internet threats from amazon.com and other large online discount distributors.

How do these companies continue to thrive? They all possess great strategies – but then so do most companies. What these three example organizations do, and do considerably well, is successfully implement.

McDonalds has standardized its operations to optimize a limited menu of products. Time and motion studies dictate the layout of the kitchen to maximize efficiency. The food is pre-measured and packaged to require minimal culinary talent in its preparation. The company hires largely unskilled frontline staff and provides only the level of training necessary to sell its food. The advertising message promoted is consistent with the product – cheap, fast, and convenient. You will not see McDonalds introduce gourmet meals or spectacular in-store dining experiences. They simply do not have the physical and intellectual assets to provide that level of quality.

Apple, oppositely, makes the superior physical design of their products an integral part of the overall design process. Design by Apple's classification includes an emphasis on compatibility and ease of use of its computers and electronics. The company has defined its customers as technology rebels. It then carries this strategy into its advertising and promotional campaigns, even mocking the established and traditional business users of technology. Recognizing itself as more of a niche player than a mass producer, the company employs a premium price structure. Apple will not be producing 50 million units of a cheap and box-like computer that requires numerous add-on products to synch it with its own peripherals. Its goal is to provide high quality technology that is up and running right out of the box.

Finally, Barnes & Noble needed a way to compete with low cost online alternatives that were rapidly driving out smaller booksellers and overpriced retailers. Rather than compete in pricing, the company instead focused its attention on the customer experience. Knowing that customers like to browse items before purchasing, Barnes & Noble added expanded onsite cafes to its extensive network of stores. This feature keeps customers in the stores and influences their making impulse purchases. The company also promotes a club membership offering special discounts (including on café items) that allows it to monitor spending patterns. Technology, in the form of multiple computer terminals at each retail location, links store inventories with Barnes & Noble's online site to provide purchasing options to customers when items are not in stock. Since retail space is expensive, the company studies purchase patterns and learns what is in demand, freeing shelf space for profitable, mass-produced bestselling books, DVDs, and CDs. You will probably not find rare or specialty textbook titles or extensive collections of old or obscure DVDs and CDs at Barnes & Noble. But that's because people don't generally buy them.

In all three of the listed examples, you may have noticed the consistency between strategy and the types of business operations used. Low cost strategies demand operations that standardize work. High quality technology products require a skilled workforce and appropriate cost structure. Customer service oriented businesses require obtaining data about customers and using that data in their product or service offerings. Strategy has an impact on the type of operational options your organization can effectively employ. Not seeing or being unable to match a strategy to the appropriate operational pieces can leave a business incapable of satisfying its customers in the marketplace.

STRATEGY ACTIVATION

Strategy Activation is the bridge that links strategy and implementation. It ensures that the promise made to the marketplace (i.e., your overarching business strategy) is fulfilled each and every day in the marketplace across every touchpoint (i.e., implementation).

The Strategy Activation model does this by driving the business strategy into the organization's key implementation elements: The Offerings, People, Processes and Tools. The model's key elements and their major components are shown in table 5.2. To clarify, the Strategy Activation model is simply a tool used to guide alignment between strategy and implementation. It identifies the key drivers of business implementation and challenges the user to think holistically and consider each and every driver when preparing to implement a strategy. Using the model as a tool, an organization can translate its strategic intent – its promise – into specific marketplace offerings (products, services, customer experiences) and the specific infrastructure needs (people, processes, tools) that can deliver both those offerings and, ultimately, the strategic intent in the marketplace.

Table 4.2—Strategy Activation Model

Each element of the model contributes in some way to marketplace implementation and is thus crucial in "getting things done." Each element must also be guided by the organization's overarching strategy or marketplace promise. When all four elements are aligned in this essential bridging capacity, connecting strategy and set of operations, it is possible to successfully meet the customers' expectations.

OFFERINGS

The first step in successful implementation of a strategy is ensuring the products and/or services you sell align with the promise you've made. If you promise great-tasting food but deliver a product that is bland and unappealing, it is unlikely your customers' expectations will be met. If you promise low prices but charge 10% more than others in the marketplace, your strategy will likely fail. If you promise world-class customer service but instead make customers listen to an endless recording of how important their call is to you, then your next promise is likely to fall on deaf ears.

The good news is most organizations get this concept. As the most visible representation of their strategy, companies have done an excellent job of aligning their products and services to their overall marketplace promise. But as products and service have become increasingly commoditized we've seen the emergence of a third and perhaps more important element of the marketplace offering – the customer experience.

The experience is the sum total of all the interactions the customer has with an organization. It goes well beyond the product itself and encompasses buying and using the product, customer service support, post-sale marketing, issue resolution, and many other factors. Your product may perform brilliantly, but if your salespeople are uninformed or rude, the negative buying experience will overshadow the product's benefits and sales will be lost.

Unfortunately today many customer experiences happen by default. That's because companies give minimal forethought to the type of experience being created. But in the next chapter we will show how to craft a well thought out series of touchpoint experiences that reinforce and fulfill the overall marketplace promise while creating competitive differentiation.

Use the simple scorecards in tables 4.3 – 4.6 below to evaluate how your organization is faring in its alignment of people with strategy. Answer the evaluative questions at the left with one of the following three choices by marking an 'X' in the appropriate box:

- **Not Done**—Indicates that no actual measurable steps to perform this activity have been undertaken.
- **WIP**—Work-In-Progress, actual measurable steps have been taken to put this item into place within the organization.
- **Completed**—The organization already does this item.

Mark the total number of 'X's in each row in the spaces for the totals.

Table 4.3—Assessing Your Organization's Offerings

Evaluative Question	Not Done	WIP	Comp
Existing products and services match the overall strategy and meet resulting customer expectations.			
Product Development teams understand the strategy and actively incorporate the promise into new products and services.			
The end-to-end customer experience has been mapped and designed to deliver the promise in each customer interaction.			
Customer feedback is monitored and analyzed to identify additional ways to improve the overall customer experience.			
TOTAL			

For Figure 4.7, copy the numbers in the Total rows of figures 4.3-4.6. Add the grand total at the end. The number of X's in each row of Figure 4.7 will tell you which areas require the most attention (i.e. the areas with most of the X's in the first column.)

PEOPLE

People truly are your organization's most important asset. They are responsible for making sure that planned actions and operational tactics intended to serve the customer are actually carried out. Because of this key role, you must look at how you attract, retain, motivate and reward personnel from the perspective that best serves the business strategy.

Do you understand what kind of people you need to conduct your business? What are the desired competencies that make a successful performer in each particular role? Do you need a service friendly workforce comfortable with interacting with the clients/customers? Is a technologically advanced skill set required of people to make unique or complex calculations? Do you require people that can work independently or need team players to populate small, focused workgroups? There are many layers to consider when defining the best workforce to suit each area within your organization. The most important aspect to remember is that your people must have or be able to acquire the knowledge, skills and abilities necessary to carry out their part of *your particular business strategy*. Do not look to replicate your competitors' methods or the model used by newly designated "world-class" companies gracing the covers of business magazines. How others hire may not be right for your purposes.

Knowing that your employees must be selected to meet your unique approach; does your human resources staff or function know what characteristics to look for in prospective employees? Does the training and development staff make sure that they are getting the best return on their training budget by teaching skills to meet strategically defined objectives and goals? Management's lack of coordination with these supporting functions risks installing a workforce that is at odds with execution and wastes time, money, and effort.

Even if you have the necessary human capital, is the company culture conducive to your business strategy? Are managers acting in the manner that they would want their subordinates to emulate when interacting with customers? Is management following company policy and demonstrating the organization's values? Employees will look to the most successful people (the leaders) in an organization to determine what actions are acceptable and to infer what the desired behavior is. Customer service organizations need the workforce at all levels to demonstrate people skills. Low cost providers need their employees to exhibit frugality in all aspects of their fiscal dealings. Leaders in technology need to support experimentation and risk taking. An organization with a culture contrary to its strategy will fight against itself, sapping motivation and ultimately causing the customer to lose out.

Support of the workforce and culture can be fostered and further bolstered by the compensation system chosen. People work for many reasons, but by far the most significant is to provide themselves and their families with steady income. Employees will therefore make sure to do those activities, actions, and tasks that are rewarded in the organization. Once a business has made the decision to pursue a particular strategy, it is paramount that the compensation and rewards system be directly aligned with meeting that strategy's key goals and objectives. The compensation system should also be robust enough to differentiate between high and low performers to boost incentive to meet targets. The truth is you get what you pay for. Make sure you pay for what you need.

Using the simple scorecard in table 4.4 below, evaluate how your organization is faring in its alignment of people with strategy.

Table 4.4—Assessing Your Organization's People

Evaluative Question	Not Done	WIP	Comp
Hiring practices and policies are designed to secure the resources required to implement the current and future company strategy.			
Training and development programs provide employees with the specific skills necessary to execute the business strategy.			
The compensation system is tied to specific goals/objectives in support of the business strategy.			
Compensation plans differentiate between high and low performers.			
Company culture supports the business strategy (leadership exemplifies the values it espouses).			
TOTAL			

PROCESSES

Processes are the series of steps the organization takes to obtain results and thereby properly deliver on the customer promise. As such, they are critical to operations. They must take into account the customer touchpoints and be designed so that these interactions provide the maximum value at each encounter. The construction of an organization's processes must relate back to the customer experience envisioned by its strategy. By aligning its workflow process to the essential experience elements, the organization is ensuring it is overtly requiring those actions and behaviors that consistently meet or surpass the customer's expectations.

We separate processes into three different types: customer facing, horizontal workflows and vertical governance. Customer facing processes guide the interactions between the company and the marketplace. They are highly visible and have a direct impact on the overall customer experience. They include activities such as marketing, sales, post-sale service, and account collections. Some customer facing processes are more subtle in their effects and can be difficult to identify. Monthly billing statements, often managed in the finance area, are an example of a customer facing process that can have a frustrating impact on the customer but is often managed strictly as an internal function.

Internal horizontal processes ensure that workflow can progress across divisions, functions and groups. To support the marketplace promise, they should emphasize outcomes as they relate to the end user or customer. Achieving strategic alignment is accomplished by removing roadblocks and redundancies while also integrating the output of multiple, parallel working teams. Horizontal processes rely heavily on the coordination and communication between fellow process workers to enable them to perform as a focused team and get the job done correctly.

Internal vertical processes establish governance and ensure that the executive-level vision is implemented down to the lowest levels of the organization. Two-way communication is paramount to achieving this goal and occurs through top-down directives and initiatives, which are balanced with bottom-up communication in the form of employee feedback. Vertical processes make sure the targeted objectives of the organization are distributed, understood and acted upon accordingly. Effective vertical processes enable an organization to rapidly effect and respond to change because information flows much smoother and faster to involved units.

Horizontal and vertical processes act in tandem throughout the organization to implement strategy. Effective process design in both types assigns explicit roles to the people performing the work. It establishes the use of measurements and tools to monitor progress and to facilitate productivity. Processes must be regularly evaluated on their ability to satisfy the customers' needs – the greatest indicator of effectiveness. Once the ability to provide for the customers' requirements is achieved, only then can processes be further refined to remove their innate inefficiencies.

Using the simple scorecard in table 4.5 below, evaluate how your organization is managing its alignment of processes with strategy.

Table 4.5— Assessing Your Organization's Processes

Evaluative Question	Not Done	WIP	Comp
Processes are focused on the customer perspective and customer experience.			
Communication and coordination channels exist across organizational divisions, functions, and workgroups.			
Internal processes are managed holistically across silos to ensure strategic alignment across the organization.			
Redundancies and non-value added tasks/steps are removed.			
Clear communication channels exist from the top organizational levels to the most subordinate employees.			
The executives and managers monitor feedback mechanisms from the lower levels of the organization.			
Processes are consistently reviewed for their impact on the overall customer experience.			
TOTAL			

TOOLS

Supporting people and processes requires tools. Tools facilitate communication and information sharing across the organization and enable the completion of specific tasks. They include everything from the low-tech pencil to the most sophisticated computer systems. E-mail, reports, databases, cash registers, selling brochures, and billing statements are all tools that enable some aspect of commerce. They are instrumental in realizing the goals of the strategy and thus the choice of tools must relate back to the marketplace promise.

Take, for example, the use of a voice recognition unit (a communication tool) to manage incoming customer calls. Does your marketplace promise demand that a live operator answer all calls or will an automated VRU satisfy customer expectations? The decision to use a VRU tool must be made in the context of your strategy and the resulting customer expectations. There are no right or wrong tools (despite what your vendors would like you to believe), only tools that enable or hinder delivery of the chosen customer experience.

STANDARDIZATION VS. CUSTOMIZATION

Every division and functional group across the organization thinks it's different and therefore needs its own unique tools. In most cases that's just not true. Every organization has some amount of repeatability, affecting everything from basic commodity products to the most customizable service. Don't reinvent the wheel. Find those elements of your business that always reoccur and analyze them to determine the most efficient manner in which they should be performed. Use this information to identify the right tools necessary to accomplish the task.

While customization may be appropriate in some instances, one must not lose sight of the broader organizational advantages of standardization. Consistent information and task tools allow employees to move seamlessly from one part of the organization to the next with less training. Standardization can also facilitate smoother corporate reorganizations, enabling whole business units and functions to integrate more easily with each other. In short, standardization can bring more organizational flexibility and consistency to operations.

TECHNOLOGY

One of the principal changes driving the choice of business tools in the past three decades is the rise of computer technology. But computer technology by itself is not a competitive advantage – every business utilizes computers. How you employ that technology is what makes the difference. Too often "cool" technology drives tool choices with little consideration given to how the tool will enable employees to satisfy the marketplace promise. Consider these questions when evaluating technology choices:

- Does the workforce know how to properly use your systems and software?
- Is technology more practical than performing the task in any other way?
- Are computers and information tracking/processing devices used at the right point in the process?
- Are your technology systems set up to work together throughout your processes?
- Does your technology serve your employees, or do your employees serve your technology?
- Does your technology support delivery of the customer experiences you've envisioned?

Choose only those technological solutions that make serving the customer more effective and efficient.

Using the simple scorecard in table 4.6 below, evaluate how your organization is proceeding in its use of tools to support strategy.

Table 4.6— Assessing Your Organization's Use of Tools and Technology

Evaluative Question	Not Done	WIP	Comp
Tool choices are reviewed in the context of the overall business strategy and envisioned customer experiences.			
Routine work is optimized for effectiveness and efficiency and supported by standardized tools across the organization.			
Technology has been integrated into work processes (where essential) to simplify steps and improve output. Its use is periodically reviewed to ensure the chosen system still aligns to the organization's strategy.			
Staff has been trained to use the organization's systems accurately. Employees see the value of the technology and use it consistently in their daily routines.			
TOTAL			

CONCLUSION

It's not what you plan to do that matters. It's how well your organization carries out its plans that truly makes an impact. What you actually accomplish is the only aspect of your business defining the customer experience – and your customers are the ones paying for your products or services.

How does your organization rate when compared to one that embraces the strategy activation model? Take a look at each of your scores for the four key element areas detailed in each previous section of this chapter: The Offerings, People, Processes and Tools. Place the total numbers for each grouping (Not Done, WIP, and Completed) into the appropriate columns in table 4.7 below. This exercise will give you a general overall assessment of your firm's current state.

Table 4.7—Your Organization's Overall Assessment

Key Element	Not Done	WIP	Comp
Offerings			
People			
Processes			
Tools			
TOTALS			

If your numbers are more skewed to the *Not Done* and *WIP* categories, fear not. The whole remainder of this book is dedicated to moving you to a strategy activation oriented organization. The subsequent chapters will deal specifically with each of the key elements of the model, breaking down the applicable specifics. You will see how to get results.

If you already have many of the characteristics of the model integrated into your organization, then bravo – you are doing quite well. The following sections will help you understand how these favorable conditions came about. More importantly, the information provided will reveal how to sustain success through an ever-changing and competitive business marketplace.

So read on – and let's start executing your strategy.

CHAPTER FIVE

PRODUCT OFFERINGS AND THE CUSTOMER EXPERIENCE

"When the product is right, you don't have to be a great marketer."
—Lee Iacocca

"A business is successful to the extent that it provides a product or service that contributes to happiness in all of its forms."
—Mihaly Csikszentmihalyi

C ustomer experiences and customer touch points shape not only customer perceptions, but company profit margins – and not always for the better.

A friend of mine named Reggie shared a relevant experience with his bank. Reggie had received an ominous fax from the bank where, just below the logo, in striking black letters, it read:

> **ACH Rules require that you make the changes specified in the NOC within six banking days or face possible fine.**

Reggie's reaction was a natural one – he was put off by the tone of the letter. He had been a good customer of this bank for a decade or so and couldn't imagine a scenario where he, as the customer, would be in a position to be fined by his bank.

He called the bank's customer service center, where the following exchange occurred:

"Hello, [bank name]," the customer service representative said.

(Reggie) "Hi there, I have a fax here that says I might get fined, but I have no idea why. Could you help?"

"Sure, what's the operational code on the fax?"

"I'm not sure what you mean."

"Do you see some numbers on the fax that say something like 3, 5, 8,..." (the customer representative read off a string of digits that did appear on the page.

"Yes, I see those... what do they mean?"

"Hold on a second..." . . . "...oh, I see. You'll have to change your TRN because we're transferring our branches to a bigger bank that brought us out."

"Wait, you just said two things," Reggie replied. "There's a number I have to change, but also, did you say something about a new bank?" Her abrupt tone had furthered flustered my friend.

"Yeah. All our branches are moving to a new bank, and their TRN is different from ours, so you have to change it." Once more, the rep's tone was a bit stand-offish.

"Sorry . . . I didn't know," Reggie said, making a mental note to close his account immediately. "And this TRN, what does that have to do with it?"

"Any money deposited in your account goes through a TRN, and so if you have the wrong number, it won't get to you."

The clouds lifting, my friend immediately understood what was going on.

"I get it now," Reggie said to the bank representative.

"You've just sold all your branches to a new bank, which needs a different code for the direct deposit of my salary. So my employer, not I, but my employer has to change where it direct-deposits my salary. Is that right?"

"That's right," the bank rep answered.

Reggie hung up. Later that same day he opened a new account at a new bank.

From my Reggie's standpoint – the customer – the experience was a disaster. The bank had threatened, insulted, and finally gave him the cold shoulder when he needed help. But what about from the bank's perspective? How did the "customer experience" rate with the bank?

A bank customer service executive concerned only with usability might consider the transaction a success, since my friend's "task success" was 100%. Reggie got the information he needed, and could not take action on the problem.

A branding executive might also feel OK about the transaction, since the bank's logo was clearly printed, according to the corporate style guide, in the upper-left corner of the page, with the correct dimensions. And the person who answered the phone clearly said the name of the bank.

The mass-marketer in the bank is probably satisfied with the bank's work, because two days later my friend received a glossy brochure in the postal mail. "Coming Soon: More convenience for you," the headline gushes, just next to the stock graphic of a man dancing with a delighted mid-air child. They fully expected Reggie to do more business with them.

From a business stand point, the customer experience was a disaster, because it gave my friend, a loyal customer of over ten years, enough reason to close his account. The fax was confusing and threatening, the long-distance phone call was flawed, and the glossy brochure, which arrived *after* the fax, was insulting in its transparency.

It's worth remembering that, in the context of the customer experience, the reality of business is the customer's reality. That's the ultimate impact of the customer experience.

CONTROLLING THE CUSTOMER EXPERIENCE

There is a positive side to the customer experience, too.

Think about it. Have you ever gone out of your way to get a cup of coffee at a specific diner/eatery because you like the way the server greets or smiles at you? Have you ever traveled further or paid a premium to visit a particular establishment because you thought favorably of its history, liked the owner's ethics, had fun there, or simply considered it the "in" spot? If your answer is "yes," the implication is that you intentionally spent additional time or money to get the exact same product or service you might have procured faster or cheaper somewhere else. Even if your answer is "no," I believe you can understand how someone could be willing to pay for something beyond the specific product or service – a positive experience.

If people are willing to pay for an experience, then it makes economic sense to give considerable attention to this aspect of your product and/or service offerings. At least it is a worthwhile strategy for those businesses that want to distinguish themselves from the competition.

Like my friend's bank story, customer experiences will happen. They happen every time your customers and prospective customers come into contact with your products/services and your company. These contacts, often called touchpoints, create the experience. The sum of all of these touchpoint experiences forms the consumers' perception of your products, your services, and your company.

Today, many of these experiences happen by default. That is, minimal forethought is given to the perception being created. In their 1999 book, *The Experience Economy: Work Is Theatre and Every Business a Stage*, B. Joseph Pine II and James H. Gilmore speak of staging experiences – crafting a well thought out series of touchpoints that establishes an overall impression, and reinforces and fulfills the overall marketplace promise while also creating competitive differentiation. To accomplish this goal, it is necessary to first understand the specific drivers of customer experience.

Bernd H. Schmitt takes this concept further in his book *Experiential Marketing – How to Get Customers to Sense, Feel, Think, Act and Relate to Your Company and Brands*. Schmitt not only talks about experiences, he also discusses some of the key drivers of those experiences.

Schmitt, like Pine and Gilmore, takes issue with the "old economy" features and benefits approach of traditional marketing. In this (traditional) model, consumers are thought to go through a considered decision-making process when evaluating a product. The potential purchaser assesses (either consciously or subconsciously) the features or characteristics of a particular product or service and perceives certain benefits in each one.

For Schmitt, however, this is far too limited a way to understand the purchase decision, with excessive emphasis on the rational and logical elements of the decision and not enough (or any) on the emotional and intuitive aspects involved in the purchase. People are not always logical or rational when making their buying decisions and can be swayed by variables outside the product itself.

Schmitt proposes a framework based upon two elements: *Strategic Experience Modules* (SEMs), which are different types of experiences, and *Experience Producers* (ExPros), which are the various agencies that deliver these experiences. Staging an experience is the discipline of creating products and services that leverage the elements of this framework.

He identifies five different types of experiences, or SEMs. These modules are:

- **Sense** – the sensual and tangible aspects of a product or experience that appeal to the five senses
- **Feel** – a marketing experience that is devoted to triggering a distinct visceral response (i.e. the creation of moods and emotions) in the customer to the company and brand
- **Think** – "The objective of think marketing is to encourage customers to engage in elaborative and creative thinking that may result in a reevaluation of the company and products."
- **Act** – marketing oriented towards the creation of experiences through the actions of the customer
- **Relate** – which expands beyond the individual's private sensations, feelings, cognitions and actions by relating the individual self to the broader social and cultural context reflected in a brand.

These five different types of experiences are created through experience touchpoints – the ExPros – and include such elements as:

- Communications, including advertising, external and internal company communications, public relations campaigns, billing statements, websites, etc.
- Visual and verbal identity and signage, including names, logos, colors, etc.

- Product presence, including design, packaging and display co-branding, and also involving event marketing, sponsorships, alliances and partnerships, licensing, product placement in movies, etc.
- Spatial environments, including the external and internal design of corporate offices, sales outlets, consumer and trade fair spaces, etc.
- People, including salespeople, company representatives, customer service providers, call center operators, etc.

The ultimate goal is to design or stage the various experience providers to create an integrated (what Schmitt calls "holistic") experience that reinforces the market promise.

THE BUSINESS IMPACT OF USING EXPERIENCE DESIGN

Taking an experience design approach forces businesses to see the world through the various perspectives of their customers and delivers new insights into how their products and services are perceived. This greater understanding should enable businesses to create more relevant and compelling propositions for their customers.

By fundamentally shifting the focus of our thinking from the products or services themselves to people's perceptions, customer experience has the power to instill a greater sense of empathy, trust and loyalty towards an organization in both customers and employees.

Embracing this paradigm will require a company to actively engineer value into its offerings and inspire the workforce.

ENGINEERING EXPERIENCE INTO YOUR OFFER

An experiential approach therefore requires businesses to "value engineer" their offer – to consciously work towards a better understanding of the aspects of their business that convey the greatest value and most positive experience to customers. This analysis is performed in tandem with the elimination of those elements that don't work or are not valued.

To bring about the "optimal customer experience" we must first address a series of key strategic questions:

- What type of holistic experience will fulfill the customer's expectations created by our marketplace promise?
- Which touchpoints are most critical to defining and delivering the holistic customer experience? (Not all touchpoints are created equal.)
- What does the experience look like at each of the critical touchpoints?
- How do we create that experience using our people, our environment, our communications, and our products and services?
- What internal cultural and infrastructural factors need to be addressed before this optimized experience can be brought to market?

The resulting customer experience that emerges from addressing such questions then becomes an integral part of a company's image.

As stated earlier, the customer experience goes beyond the products and services an organization sells. Done well it can provide a "wow" factor that attracts the attention of both customers and the media. Consistent delivery of an optimized experience for a particular strategy will span an enormous spectrum – how and where you advertise, what your salesman says, ease of product setup, how issues are resolved, to name just a few.

Experience design enhances the overall value of products and/or services, creating a stronger and often more premium-priced offering. Customers sometimes want more than the act of simply selecting, purchasing, and taking home a product or service when they shop. Department stores, for example, are increasingly offering personal shopping and lifestyle consultants. Customers that choose to shop at such establishments are clearly making a decision to invest in an integrated solution to their shopping needs. They want the perceived added value of emotional stimuli, additional interactions, and positive memories during a purchase, and they are willing to pay the increased cost to get them.

As companies tap into the emerging experiential economy, consumers' expectations of branded experiences will become more sophisticated and demanding. Businesses will need to more fully incorporate Schmitt's five distinct experience types as central components of their long-term customer experience planning. Formal planning of customer experiences will be a requirement, not an option in the new competitive landscape, assuming this mindset is evidenced to help businesses keep in touch with ever-increasing consumer expectations about what constitutes acceptable and valued customer experiences.

INSPIRING YOUR EMPLOYEES

In order to credibly deliver on the total consumer promise and the resulting envisioned customer experience, it is also becoming increasingly important that the internal employees' experience be coherent, compelling and in line with what's offered to a company's customers.

In doing so, companies are recognizing the necessity for all of their people to "live the brand" by developing internal programs and cultural change initiatives that are designed to turn strategic brand values into predominant behaviors.

Employees need to fully understand that this approach entails a shift in focus from performing "tasks" simply to fulfill the obligations of their job description to envisioning what the customers actually experience. Understanding, however, is just the fist step. As we progress through the book, you will see how employees need the support of the organization's processes and tools to deliver positive customer experiences. Inspiration has many sources.

In the final decades of the last century we witnessed the emergence of the "service economy." The commoditization of the product driven by fierce competition, reverse engineering, and shortened development cycles brought down the product-based barriers to entry and made it more difficult for manufacturers to maintain meaningful differentiation in the marketplace. Companies increasingly wrapped their products in differentiating services (e.g. free training, financing options, and superior after-sales service) to attract and retain customers. As new categories emerged, products began to take a backseat to service. Consider the mobile phone industry, which was all too happy to give us a free phone as a gateway to selling us long-term telephone service contracts. The business press overflowed with books and articles heralding the rise of the service economy.

Pine and Gilmore recognize in the *The Experience Economy* that even services that once differentiated competitors are becoming commoditized. They hypothesize that this new reality is driving the emergence of the next phase of economic evolution: the Experience Economy.

According to Pine and Gilmore, *"An experience is not an amorphous construct; it is as real an offering as any service, good, or commodity."* Yet the experience goes beyond any individual product or service drawing on the personal interactions between customer and vendor.

Still, we need a concrete definition of what an experience is. Fortunately, Pine and Gilmore provide one when they say, *"While prior economic offerings – commodities, goods, and services – are external to the buyer, experiences are inherently personal, existing only in the mind of an individual who has been engaged on an emotional, physical, intellectual, or even spiritual level."*

What this means is that an experience is the entirety of the interactions between a business and its customers. Furthermore, it is also the impression (positive or negative) that is left in the minds of the customers as a direct result of these exchanges.

YOU WON'T BELIEVE THIS – STORIES OF SERVICE FAILURE

Despite all of the promises and service guarantees espoused by modern business, many organizations are still missing the boat when it comes to truly understanding their customer's perspective. It seems almost everyone has heard an amusing or downright disturbing anecdote or two detailing a poor customer experience. I am no different, as the following two stories can attest. Cringe if you must.

WHAT ONE HAND GIVES, THE OTHER HAND TAKES BACK

A few years ago my family had the misfortune of having our house robbed twice in less than a year. Both times a thief smashed a first floor bedroom window while we were away on vacation and took what he could carry. Given the similar circumstances, we were pretty sure it was one perpetrator who decided to come back for seconds. Unfortunately, the police were never able to catch the thief, who presumably walks the streets today a free man, though hopefully with a guilty conscience. (To any other would-be thieves out there, don't bother with our house. There's nothing left!)

But this isn't a story about society's ills. It's a story about homeowner's insurance. Up until this time we had owned homes for 16 years without ever making an insurance claim. We spent all 16 of those years with the same industry-leading, national insurance company and represented by the same agent.

We're all told insurance companies are very good at taking your money but impossible to deal with when you need some back. Much to my surprise, our claims experiences proved to be quite the opposite. The adjustors and customer service people we dealt with were compassionate, empathetic, and very fair. In fact, after our second incident, a quirk of our policy precluded part of our claim. To make up for this shortfall, the adjustor waived our $1,000 deductible, thus giving us more than they were technically obligated. I was stunned. Even delighted. I told the story to everyone I knew. I was now a raving fan of my insurance company. How many people do you know who rave about their insurance company?

The honeymoon ended three weeks later, however, when I received a form letter from my insurance company informing me that after reviewing my claims history they would no longer be able to offer me homeowner's insurance. I had to read the letter three times before I fully comprehended that I was being dumped. After the adjustors bent over backwards to make me a satisfied customer, the underwriters were tossing me out on my ear.

Believing there must have been a mistake, I called my agent, who had been uncomfortably silent throughout this entire process.

He confirmed that he too had received the letter and that, yes, my policy would not be renewed. I was struck by his cavalier attitude. Granted we hadn't been close over the years, but I had been a loyal client for 16 years. You'd think that commitment would have at least merited a phone call.

The only consolation the agent offered was that despite the loss of the homeowner's coverage, there was no effect on the other five policies I had with him. Like he was doing me a favor! But customer relationships don't work that way. Once burned, trust is lost. My agent and his company exposed their true colors, and I had no desire to continue my relationship. I moved my entire business to another company – and saved a significant amount of money in the process.

I love this story because it illustrates both the complexity of a customer experience and the range of factors involved. In this case the agent, the adjustors, and the underwriters each had a different role to play in the overall customer experience. Yet the experience itself was defined by the whole. The heroic actions of the adjustors were negated by the callous interpretation of the underwriting policy and the lack of communication from the agent. The result was the dissolution of a solid 16-year customer relationship.

POLICY OVER PEOPLE

Because of my extensive work in customer experience design and implementation, friends and acquaintances love to share their own customer experience nightmares with me. It never ceases to amaze me how good companies can easily and effectively destroy a customer relationship.

Recently my friend Dave related the following story. Many years ago his wife succumbed to cancer and passed on into the next world. They were a couple deeply in love and shared a very close relationship. The loss was devastating to both my friend and his young daughter.

A couple of weeks after the funeral, Dave found himself in the awkward position of having to inform his bank that his wife had passed and that he needed to remove her name from his accounts. After offering the appropriate expressions of condolence, the bank made the changes.

A week later Dave received a letter from the bank informing him that his mortgage had to be refinanced immediately. Given the fact that both he and his wife were part of the original underwriting process, the bank's *policy* was to call the note. Dave had to refinance as a single applicant. So in the middle of his grieving process, Dave had to go through the process of refinancing his home. (Anyone who's applied for a mortgage knows this isn't a fun process under the best of circumstances.)

Take a guess at how Dave now feels about this bank? How long do you think he remained a customer?

Here's a newsflash: your customers don't care about your *policies*. They care about their needs and whether those needs are being met in a satisfying way. Too often companies hide behind their policies in the belief that they ensure fair and equal treatment of customers while maintaining an appropriate return on their products. But as we move deeper into the experience economy, these very same policies more often than not will drive customers away. Why? Because they are not attuned to the company's marketplace promise and thus create unintended negative customer experiences.

THE CUSTOMER EXPERIENCES THE COMPANY THROUGH ITS TOUCHPOINTS

There is a strong positive correlation between the complexity of the product and the importance of the customer experience. Consider the purchase of a consumer cake mix. The experience is relatively straightforward. You go to the grocery store, select a flavor, choose a brand, shell out $1.49, bring it home, bake it up, and eat it. It tastes good, end of experience. The entire ordeal is measured in days.

Compare that relatively simple example above to purchasing a mortgage for your home. Despite the commoditization of the mortgage industry, the product choices are maddeningly complex. The application (i.e. purchase) process is no less daunting.

Think about the steps a customer must go through to purchase a mortgage. There's the initial contact with a home mortgage consultant and the selection of an appropriate product. This stage is followed by the application process, which may include the submission of reams of highly personal financial documentation. This part of the process is often managed by an operations specialist. Once documentation is complete, we move to the decision process managed by the underwriting group. If the underwriters reach a favorable decision, they schedule a closing, which is often managed by a third party closer. Post-closing the loan needs to be onboarded. Onboarding involves welcoming the new customer and setting up the payment and escrow processes. This entire purchase experience is measured in weeks or even months.

The total experience, however, doesn't end at that point. This same mortgage product may be owned for years. During that time the customer may call customer service representatives to make inquiries or address perceived issues. Additionally, the bank may try to cultivate a deeper relationship by cross-selling other products it offers, including deposit accounts, investment services, or even insurance.

Every single one of these "events" represents a customer touchpoint – a moment in time when the customer comes in contact with the bank. Taken together, these points of contact define the overall customer experience. A significant breakdown at any one of the touchpoints can leave such a bad taste in customers' mouths that they will choose to go to a competitor the next time they need a mortgage. Or worse yet, they'll tell everyone they know how bad their bank is.

Complicating this issue is the sheer number of people touching the customer. There's the mortgage consultant, the documentation specialist, the underwriter, the closer, the onboarding specialist, and the ongoing contacts with customer service reps. In a large organization, these positions represent thousands of employees creating the customer experience on a daily basis. And in addition to the employees there are the tools used – the mortgage application, the legal disclaimers, the communication vehicles (e.g. phone, fax, e-mail), the monthly statements, etc.

The mortgage example illustrates the touchpoints in a typical B2C relationship. The emphasis is on a single decision maker (the consumer) whom we touch multiple times in the business relationship. Identifying and managing touchpoints in a B2B relationship is a bit different but no less important. In a B2B relationship we place more emphasis on the many decision makers and users that must be satisfied if the relationship is to continue. For example, if we're selling an employee health insurance program to a large corporation, there are several stakeholders, each with their own customer expectations. The primary buying decision may involve purchasing, finance, HR, and senior management. Once the initial sale is made, servicing the account will involve the end users and the employees, as well as HR and/or finance. Each stakeholder has different needs and experiences your product from a different perspective. In this example we would look at senior management, purchasing, finance, HR, and the employees as different touch-points. (In Chapter 9 we will present a B2B case study. Comparing that study to the B2C example below should clarify the different approaches.)

Only recently have organizations come to realize that the customer experience can't be left to chance. It needs to be aggressively managed. It needs to be aligned to the marketplace promise and the customer expectations that promise creates. Remember that we said that the company differentiates itself by making a promise to the marketplace. **The customer is the only one who gets to decide if that promise is being kept.** More often than not, the overall experience the customer has with an organization – the summation of each individual experiences across all of the touch-points – determines if he or she is satisfied and chooses to remain a customer. All too often, the product itself becomes secondary.

So how does one actively manage the customer experience? It starts by envisioning the optimal experience. What kind of experience do you want to deliver at each touchpoint? Once you know what experience you're striving toward, then you must align the infrastructure – people, processes and tools – to the delivery of that experience at each and every touchpoint each and every day.

WEBEFINE MORTGAGE EXAMPLE

Let's talk about envisioning a customer experience one step at a time. To do this we will create our own mythical mortgage company. We'll call it WeBeFine Mortgage. After researching the competitive landscape, we've determined that there's an opportunity to demystify, simplify, and humanize the mortgage process. Thus we have established our Marketplace Promise:

Our Promise
WeBeFine Mortgage simplifies the mortgage process.

Our research shows that this is a promise that will resonate with 56 percent of all current homeowners and 82 percent of renters that are would-be homeowners. Those percentages show how daunting the current process is and how hungry consumers are for an easier, more straightforward process.

How are we going to simplify the mortgage process? Why should prospective customers believe this promise? What are we going to actually do that's different from what other mortgage companies do? These questions form the pillars of our promise. Our research has helped us define three pillars:

WeBeFine's Pillars

1) **Personalized Service** – We are the customer's advocate and will guide them the whole way through.

2) **Continuous Communication** – Our customers will always know where we are in the process and what to expect going forward.

3) **Straightforward Documentation** – We have minimized documentation requirements and converted much of our legal copy to plain language for ease of customer use and understanding.

Again, our research shows that if we can deliver on this promise through the three identified pillars, then our little mortgage company will be a runaway success. How can we be sure that the customers truly experience personalized service, continuous communication, and straightforward documentation every time they encounter WeBeFine Mortgage? The simple answer is we need to carefully craft the customer experience at each touchpoint in the process. We need to envision a complete experience that, when implemented properly, truly results in a painless mortgage process.

We must begin by tracing our commercial processes and identify all of the customer touchpoints. Some of these touchpoints are more obvious than others. For example, the touchpoint between mortgage consultant and prospective customers during "*Initial Contact*" is obvious. The touchpoint created by the monthly mortgage statement during "*Servicing*" and its effect on the overall experience may be less obvious.

A simple trace of the mortgage acquisition and servicing process yields the following touchpoints (Figure 5.2):

Figure 5.2— Mortgage Acquisition Process

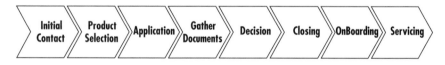

Buried within each of these process steps are the elements that determine the customer experience – whether we are living up to our promise. For example, at the point of "*Application*" there are the behaviors of our mortgage consultants, the complexity of the application document, the customer process for completing the documentation requirements, etc. Similarly, "*Servicing*" includes the behaviors of our customer service reps, our monthly statements, the customer process for getting issues and questions addressed, etc.

We must ensure that at each point in the process above, we are living up to our promise. To accomplish this, we must translate our pillars into specific behaviors and outcomes at each point that will lead to the desired customer experience. We call this translation envisioning the customer experience. It begins with the creation of a simple matrix (Figure 5.3):

Figure 5.3—Mortgage Acquisition Matrix

	Initial Contact	Product Selection	Application	Gather Documents	Decision	Closing	OnBoarding	Servicing
Personalized Service								
Over-Communication								
Straightforward Documentation								

The matrix facilitates our visioning process. Each box in the matrix should list the explicit experience that ensures that specific pillar is realized at that particular point in the commercial process. Let's take a look at the *"Product Selection"* element as an example.

1) **What does providing Personalized Service mean during *"Product Selection?"***

    WeBeFine Mortgage will take the time to understand our prospective clients, assess their individual borrowing needs, their attitudes toward money management, and their appetites for financial risk. We encourage these meetings to take place face-to-face, either in our office or at the customers' homes if so desired. Based on these discussions, we will develop a list of three potential products we believe will meet their individual needs. We will carefully explain all the features, benefits, and pros and cons of each product in plain language they can understand.

2) What does providing Continuous Communication mean during *"Product Selection?"*

WeBeFine will ensure that every customer completely understands all the features, benefits, and pros and cons of each product we recommend. We will sit with the customer until he/she feels they understand what is being offered. When they leave, they will carry with them clearly worded sell sheets that describe the products in detail and offer useful comparisons between the products. Three days after the products are presented, we will follow up by phone to see if there are any lingering product questions we can answer.

3) What does providing Straightforward Documentation mean during *"Product Selection?"*

All WeBeFine products will be clearly described in plain language. Wherever legal disclaimers are required by law, the purpose and meaning of each disclaimer will be outlined using only straightforward language. Nothing about the product will remain clouded in legalese.

As you can see from these examples, we have touched on various experiential elements. We addressed employee behaviors (spending time assessing customer needs), processes (meeting face-to-face and following up by phone), and supporting tools (providing plain language sell sheets.) As you will see in the chapters that follow, these elements – people, processes and tools – are the elements that will ultimately determine whether we live up to our promise and establish our success or failure in the marketplace.

Once all the boxes in the matrix have been addressed and filled in we will have designed the optimal customer experience, one that should ultimately take the fear out of the mortgage process and fulfill the marketplace promise.

CONCLUSION

Products and services have become commoditized. The new competitive advantage comes from recognizing the importance of customers' experiences. These are the often overlooked emotional and psychological perceptions associated with customer touch-points that will cumulatively forge an impression in the customers' minds. Whether this impression is ultimately positive or negative is subject to how well a business understands and plans for these interactions ahead of time. Make no mistake: favorable experiences are something the marketplace is willing to pay for. They also serve to differentiate one company's products or services from another when their basic attributes are almost identical.

Capitalizing on this new experience economy will not be easy. It specifically requires businesses to employ a strategy focused on the true demands of the marketplace and then take the necessary and proper internal actions to align the organization's people, processes, and tools to meet the opportunity.

CHAPTER SIX

PEOPLE MAKE THE DIFFERENCE

"Motivate them, train them, care about them and make winners out of them... they'll treat the customers right. And if customers are treated right, they'll come back."
—J. Marriott Jr.

"Good management consists in showing average people how to do the work of superior people."
—John D. Rockefeller

INTRODUCTION

Most businesses proclaim that their people are their greatest asset, whether or not they truly believe it. Your people are indeed important; they actually perform the work.

One of the single biggest issues hampering implementation of a company's strategy is its employees' lack of understanding of what is expected from their role. The vast majority of companies just do not communicate their stratagem broadly throughout the organization, or they simply communicate using pithy t-shirt slogans (*"Quality is Job #1," "Spirit of Service," "Customer Focused," "To Be the Best"*) that leave too much open to interpretation. The employees are left to guess how the marketplace promise applies to their daily work.

Remove the guesswork; it's inefficient and provides you with absolutely no tangible advantage. Show your employees where and how they need to contribute their talents.

Motivate your people to do the right things for themselves, the organization, and the customer. The three do not need to be mutually exclusive.

How can you accomplish all of these things? Understand and build your organization's competencies and install a compensation plan and reward structure to encourage the correct behaviors.

Taking these actions will help you develop, communicate, and maintain a culture focused on consistently delivering on the marketplace promise.

COMPETENCIES

Once a strategy is carefully analyzed, planned, and crafted, it still remains just an idea, a concept that needs to be fulfilled in the marketplace.

People are integral to your realizing a strategy that delivers for the customer. They are the only components that actively drive the execution.

Assessing and understanding the value of your human capital is therefore quite essential. Only when you know honestly what you have can you determine whether you already possess a sufficient workforce, one that requires additional training, if you need to import new talent, or if you can use a combination of tactics.

Assessing your workforce's competencies requires management to actively coordinate with the organization's human resources/ recruitment and development departments.

Take a look at each of your business processes as they are derived from the strategy. You have already identified the touchpoints, pillars, and the key components that define how to deliver the optimal customer experience. List the specific minimum knowledge, skills, and abilities (KSAs) required to perform the elements for each touchpoint.

- **Knowledge:** refers to a body of attributes and information required to perform a task that is usually gained through focused education, service, or training.
- **Skills:** refer to proficiency with psychomotor acts that can be manual, verbal, or mental manipulation.
- **Abilities:** refer to the power to perform an observable activity (plan, organize, and lead) resulting in a desired tangible product or service.

Now compare the KSAs required to deliver the envisioned customer experience at each touchpoint with the qualifications of the employees working at each one (or moving into a position at one). Also look at employees whose role is to support the customer-facing workers. Do your employees possess the appropriate capabilities?

If the answer is yes, then you know you at least have a work-force competent enough to carry out the strategy. If there is a gap, then you must assess whether the employees falling short should be replaced, transitioned to areas more suited to their level, or if they have the aptitude to obtain the proper qualifications through training or development options.

One of my own experiences as a General Manager clearly illustrates the need to match the right employee with the right job:

Following an acquisition, I was faced with the task of integrating two small lawn care companies into a single organization. Each company had its own sales team run by a Vice President of Sales. The newly formed entity required only one field sales leader. A choice had to be made.

Rather than lose a talented sales veteran I created a new sales strategy position. This position was responsible for translating our marketplace promise into solid selling plans and creating the necessary tools to support our selling efforts. Thus Steve was appointed VP of Field Sales and Jerry was appointed VP of Sales Planning and Implementation.

It seemed like the perfect solution.

Six months later I found myself dealing with two personnel challenges. Steve lacked the people skills necessary to run a larger sales team and was more interested in criticizing the plans and tools coming out of Jerry's sales planning area. Unfortunately that criticism was well founded. Jerry lacked strategic insight and creativity. He was clearly a better field general than a strategist and planner.

The solution was obvious. Steve and Jerry were both in the wrong jobs. So I switched them. Jerry was appointed VP of Field Sales and Steve took over as VP of Sales Planning and Implementation. Improvement was instantaneous. Both Jerry and Steve flourished in their new roles and the effectiveness of the sales organization increased dramatically.

DEVELOPMENT

Another "people issue" that consistently comes up in Strategy Activation is employee development. In many cases, employees will be asked to reasonably "stretch" what they're capable of in order to meet the demands of the new strategy.

To increase the competencies of your workforce requires a well-organized development program. A development program that adds value should provide training programs and access to mentoring. It should also plan and monitor employee growth.

To be an effective tool in support of strategy, all training should reinforce delivery of the chosen marketplace promise. It should incorporate specific examples and scenarios of situations commonly encountered within the company and describe the correct or accepted best approaches for resolving these issues.

One way to accomplish this is to glorify company "legends" by recounting stories of heroic and successful efforts that drive the company's overarching strategy and build its envisioned image in the marketplace.

Consider, for example, the positive impact on new and existing employees of this story related to me by a friend who works at a large food service supply company. I call it "The Legend of the Dishwashing Caravan."

As part of their promise to help their customers maintain a smooth operation my friend's company distributes and maintains dishwashing equipment and supplies to hotels and restaurants across the country. As one might expect, the breakdown of a dishwasher can be catastrophic for any food service operation that uses anything but disposable plates, glasses and flatware.

One Saturday night, Jim, an account manager, received a panicked call on his cell from the manager of, a large hotel that was part of a well-known chain. Apparently one of the dishwashers had just failed.

The hotel had four major events scheduled and every ballroom and meeting space was filled to capacity. There was no way the hotel would be able to wash their dishes quickly enough to serve all of these hungry revelers in a timely fashion.

A quick assessment revealed that there was no way the dishwasher could be repaired in time to support the night's festivities so Jim started making calls. He discovered that a property, just 20 miles away and owned by the same chain had excess dishwashing capacity.

So Jim rounded up a few account managers and they went to work. For the next several hours they made the 40 mile round trip taking away racks and racks of dirty dishes, glasses and utensils and returning with clean ready-to-use place settings.

At the end of the night the effort was dubbed a huge success. All of the hotel's functions went off without a hitch. The customer was eternally grateful. And Jim and his fellow account managers became corporate legends

Here's a final word about training: When training is outsourced, the trainers may not have the same focus and values that are required by your company strategy. The development team needs to closely monitor or collaborate with outside providers to ensure the content of programs is consistent with the internal strategy and that its message is consistent.

Another method to help employees stretch their capabilities, and a first cousin to training, is mentoring.

Mentoring, where lower level individuals are paired with senior members of your firm, affords the opportunity for employees to learn the finer subtleties of your organization and its culture. Experienced general managers can coach younger managers through the unwritten rules and requirements that tend to determine advancement.

In this way younger employees are exposed to someone that can guide them on how to exemplify the firm's values and ethics, assist them with communicating effectively, and give them a safe platform for receiving feedback and constructive criticism.

Mentoring allows your current leaders to shape the future ones.

Planning and monitoring the growth of employees is critical to ensuring that they are exposed to important information and contacts, and that they encounter essential experiences over time in a progressively challenging and structured manner. Accomplishing this task involves taking the time and effort to rationally assign training opportunities for obtaining new competencies, matching people to the right mentors, and rotating your employees through projects and/or duties in a logical manner to expand their roles. These critical assignments should not be made arbitrarily. It is your workforce. Guiding employees' progression serves to increase your organizations' potential while communicating to them their value. This is also a potent method of retention, since employees can see a clear path to advancement and feel supported in reaching their career goals.

Assessing and developing an organization's competencies is an ongoing process. As strategy is changed or updated, the workforce must be evaluated, shortfalls identified, and resource issues addressed. Consider the example that follows.

THE CABLE GUY(S)

A friend of mine once told me that hating one's cable company is one of the inalienable rights guaranteed by our constitution. I failed to understand this sentiment until my local cable service was taken over by large national competitor. Simultaneous to this transition I upgraded from standard cable to high definition digital cable.

Had I known at the time that high definition digital cable signals are much more persnickety than standard cable signals perhaps I would have made a different decision. After all, we only watch a handful of shows each week. But everyone else seemed to be taking the plunge so we decided to jump into the deep end of the pool.

Installation was a snap and within mere minutes we had crisp images to "ooh" and "ahh" at.

Until the next day. The high definition channels were unviewable.

The cable company scheduled a service call. The technician informed me that my signal strength was too low. He tinkered with a few settings, tested the line and said we were good to go.

Two weeks later the same problem returned, resulting in something called tiling. Up to that point, I thought that was something you did to the bathroom floor. Another service call was scheduled. This time the technician ran a new cable up from the street. He tinkered with a few settings, tested the line and said everything was fine.

Thirty days later the HD channels were tiling again. Another call and another service technician. This time, however, I was smart enough to report the problem as chronic and I got one of their lead service technicians. He explained the more demanding nature of the HD signal. He also mentioned that my new cable company's technicians didn't have a firm grasp on the technology they had acquired from my previous cable provider and thus repeat and chronic problems were on the rise.

This didn't do much to raise my confidence level.

After telling me that the previous technician was an idiot he tinkered with a few settings, tested the line and said my system was working.

I know this will surprise you, but three weeks later the problem returned.

I was now out of patience. I got into my car and drove to the cable company's retail store two suburbs over. I frostily recounted my experience thus far.

The rep looked at me with sad eyes, shrugged and simply said, "I know. We suck don't we? If I were you I'd write a letter to complain."

My signal problem remains unresolved as I recount this story.

My cable company clearly failed to give their local service technicians the competencies necessary to address problems with their newly acquired technology. This likely increased costs (due to frequent revisits) and left both customers and employees frustrated.

One final note regarding the subject of competency: If an honest assessment of capabilities reveals a need to completely remake your organization in order to fulfill the promise, you've chosen the wrong promise.

Strategy Activation is not about blowing up the existing infrastructure (workforce and systems) and building a completely new one from scratch. That option is too disruptive, high risk, and extremely time intensive. Instead we want to leverage and mold the existing infrastructure through enhancements and additions that create the necessary support for the promise. That means starting with a promise that is within reach of your current organization.

CULTURE

Every organization has an internal culture, whether you actively develop it or not. For example Apple and Ferrari are committed to innovative product design. Ritz Carlton and Nordstrom focus on customer interactions. Wells Fargo and Chase are dedicated to financial safety and security. All of these companies are very successful yet have very different corporate cultures.

There are no good or bad cultures, only cultures that either support or hinder delivery of a company's professed marketplace promise.

Don't leave the culture to develop through chance. You can decide whether your culture will be a positive, powerful force that enables your company to perform at its highest levels, or if it will become a negative, overwhelming obstacle that must constantly be overcome to get anything of significance accomplished.

Culture is comprised of shared values and norms (informal accepted standards of behavior) common to the majority of the workforce. It permeates deeply and goes beyond those items that are expressly written or espoused as company values and documented in procedures and conduct manuals. It encompasses the more subtle qualities implicit in the observable actions of the people, the emphasis inherent in the compensation system, and the priorities and types of messages communicated through the company's formal and informal channels.

The most important aspect of a corporate culture is this: **Culture shapes and coordinates behaviors, particularly what individuals prioritize and the types of decisions they make.** The type of culture you foster will ultimately determine how your organization executes. Additionally, and just as important, a strong positive culture can energize and motivate people. It strengthens their desire to accomplish something meaningful.

Who wouldn't want that attitude from his or her employees?

How do you develop a culture focused on fulfilling your unique customer promise in the marketplace?

The answer is not simple, but there are several key factors influencing culture that you can control.

- Hire only those employees that can commit themselves to your strategy and that are capable of performing the specific role set forth for their position.
- Communicate a consistent internal message celebrating fulfillment of the customer promise.
- Walk the talk – reinforce commitment to the strategy through visible management actions.

– Design a compensation plan and system of rewards that motivates and recognizes behavior that enables the company to deliver on the marketplace promise.

HIRE AND DEVELOP A COMMITTED WORKFORCE

Whether you are hiring to fortify the current workforce or to enable expansion, make it a requirement of the process that candidates exhibit defined characteristics that fit with your strategic vision and preferred culture before being given consideration. If your promise is to deliver the lowest prices to consumers you want executives that have demonstrated a keen ability to drive costs down. Executives who have spent the bulk of their careers building luxury brands might not transition well to a cost conscious culture.

Skills may be taught and experience gained, but it is much harder and more time consuming to alter someone's ideology to match your own. No matter how talented an individual, when someone does not believe in or support the organization's efforts, that person will eventually become a distraction at best and a counterproductive liability at worst. An employee that is not aligned with your strategic priorities provides an obstacle to those that are. Incompatibility destroys relationships from the inside out. Avoid this problem all together by looking for a cultural fit upfront.

CLEARLY COMMUNICATE THE PROMISE

Sell the goal of delivering on the marketplace promise internally to your organization. Sell it in a planned and thoughtful manner to convey its importance. Everyone hears that organizational communication is important to the success of any business.

The problem is that this statement has become so generic that it has lost any meaningful value.

The external marketplace promise made to the customer must be understood internally by the workforce. This is the biggest communication challenge management has.

If your people do not know what the customer's expectations are, they cannot reasonably be expected to successfully fulfill them.

To accept a disparity here is to acknowledge that guesswork is an appropriate implementation methodology, and we know that's not acceptable. Therefore, let employees know what the customer knows (and then some).

Most important to the success of your communications is to eliminate contradiction. Messages that are transmitted and received at different organizational levels or units cannot be at odds with each other. If procurement is pursuing a low price strategy and product development is pursuing an innovative design strategy, conflict and dysfunction are bound to result.

Conflicting information is inefficient, creates uncertainty, and diminishes the impact and usefulness of future efforts. Contradictions demotivate people at best; at worst they lead to inaction or incorrect actions, which are of no benefit to anyone. Don't put your people in positions where they can't rely on their information or they are forced to make critical decisions based on mixed messages.

WALK THE TALK

In addition to formal communications, it is important to recognize that there are informal communications that carry just as much weight when it comes to influencing behavior and shaping culture.

These are the underlying messages implicit in management's actions.

A manager may say that balancing sales growth across the entire product portfolio is a key goal. But in weekly staff meetings, if all he asks for is sales figures for the top three products, he is implicitly communicating to his team that sales for the rest of the product line are secondary.

Any attempts to drive a particular marketplace strategy can be severely undermined if employees are continually exposed to activities at odds with stated goals. People will observe what management does and adjust their behavior and priorities accordingly.

REWARD DESIRED BEHAVIORS

Think about your compensation system. What are employees required to do to maximize their own financial returns? Is this arrangement consistent with the very best way to fulfill the customer promise?

If there is an inconsistency, you'd better believe personal concerns will take priority over customer concerns. That's simply a fact of human nature. Don't make your employees decide between the business strategy and maximizing their own return. Make both aims consistent with each other.

Create a reward structure that pays for meeting the specific job/position duties that optimally drive the marketplace promise. Doing so communicates a strong internal message about where your commitment lies.

We'll cover the methods to align compensation systems and some successful practices for delivering rewards in further detail in the *next* section.

A KINDER, GENTLER CULTURE

In the opening chapter of the book we referenced some customer service issues at the telecommunications giant Qwest that ultimately led to a change in strategy. More specifically, in 2002 Qwest had to answer some very nasty charges brought by the Attorney General of the State of Colorado.

According to the Denver Post between January 2001 and June 2002 the office of the Colorado Attorney General received more than 3,700 complaints from Qwest customers. Several hundred of these complaints alleged high-pressure or misleading sales tactics. As a result the AG brought action against Qwest under that state's Consumer Protection Law.

As the article goes on to say, some believe that the fast-moving growth mentality preached by senior Qwest leadership trickled down to the sales departments where it was interpreted as pressure to build sales by any means possible.

While Qwest never admitted to committing the illegal acts alleged by the attorney general's office, they were forced to sign a consent decree, under threat of court-imposed penalties, promising not to:

- Bill customers for services never ordered.
- Refuse to let customers return unwanted products or cancel unwanted services.
- Tell new customers they had to buy expensive feature bundles to get basic phone service.

While we may never know precisely what happened at Qwest, it seems clear that a counter-productive sales culture developed. Qwest's marketplace promise certainly never involved questionable sales practices or angering customers. Yet one can easily imagine how pressure from above to make the numbers (and a reward system tied directly to those numbers) might override any other strategy communications.

METRICS AND REWARDS

Compensation and rewards play a large part in the success of an organization. Both have the ability to significantly shape culture and drive desired organizational behaviors.

It is human nature to maximize our financial and non-financial rewards, and that's what people tend to do. **The statement "you get what you pay for" is never truer than when dealing with your employees.** Therefore, it is not only important to identify and tell people what you want; in order to provide legitimacy for your desired outcomes, you must also take the next step and integrate them into your compensation and rewards system

Everything we say we want employees to do can be completely undone by a compensation system that favors conflicting behaviors.

As we saw earlier, we may tell customer service reps that we want them to take the time necessary to understand and resolve customer complaints. But if we then reward them solely on the number of calls they complete per day, we are creating dissonance.

Employees always make their own inferences and draw conclusions about what is important by following where the money goes and watching who gets promoted. When management gives away more money, praise, and opportunities to people performing item 'A,' you will not get people to spend their time and efforts to perform item 'B.' Even when you explicitly tell people to do item 'B' through memos, slogans, meetings, job descriptions, and change programs, as long as doing item 'A' provides more financial and career incentives, you will have conflict.

MEASURING THE RIGHT STUFF

Einstein once said, "Not everything that can be counted counts, and not everything that counts can be counted." All too often today, compensation and rewards are based on internal operational targets (e.g. profit, cost reduction, productivity – think of these as the point "A") that have little or no bearing on the promise made to the marketplace (think of this promise as point "B").

This situation primarily arises as the result of business tradition and the inability or lack of sufficient inertia to force a view of compensation from an entire systems perspective (i.e. looking at the whole company as one integrated system as opposed to relying on individual operational components and their targets). Therefore, it is essential to align how we measure and reward behaviors so that the specific activities that drive successful implementation receive the majority of the rewards.

To do this, we need to know how to move from a focus on traditional number targets to those emphasizing the satisfaction of customer expectations – moving from point "A" to point "B," in other words.

Useful metrics are numerical measures and established targets that will tell if key processes are working properly to deliver on the marketplace.

By tell I mean that the numbers give a clear indication of whether the organization's actions are effective or not and also set specific goals to achieve. Think about two different measures, for example, such as the number of widgets produced and the number of successfully filled widget orders. The first number only describes productivity, but as any manager knows, producing something does not mean that it will be sold. The second measure directly relates back to the marketplace. Any number less than

100 percent indicates that improvement is possible (and necessary). It conveys more useful and actionable information.

The most dangerous aspect of setting metrics is creating unintended consequences.

We often challenge our clients to look at what the outcome would be if all the metrics chosen were achieved. Take a sample order for a product or service and run it through the process. Will meeting each established metric ensure that the product or service satisfies the marketplace promise (and does it do so optimally)? If not, then it is time to go back and reassess the metrics, adding any missing ones and/or deleting any extraneous ones. We suggest repeating the process until you have a system of measurements that clearly allows you to view your actual marketplace performance and that provides enough information to make knowledgeable adjustments.

FINANCIAL COMPENSATION

We now know we have to structure employee monetary compensation so that it is focused on paying for strategy-oriented results.

How can we do this? We return to the touchpoints in the delivery process, the points that directly affect the customer. When you define the touchpoints and create the matrix envisioning the customer experience as we did in *Chapter 4*, you specifically write out the pillars and the elements that are required to meet customer expectations. This enables us to create a specific and comprehensive list of tasks for each employee that affect marketplace implementation at the touchpoints.

Through experience, I have found that employees will have on average three to five critical tasks that they must perform routinely to ensure proper execution of their role. Since the critical tasks are based on fulfilling the promise at the touchpoints derived from the marketplace strategy, we are delineating actions that deliver on that strategy. This creates the foundation for a meaningful and effective rewards structure.

Take the time to clearly define what successful completion means for each task with each employee. Provide examples of common scenarios showing how a model employee would accomplish them. Use quantitative targets to accurately show what must be reached. *The successful completion of these tasks is where all or a majority of the employees compensation should now be directed.*

Pay for performance that delivers on the promise. Avoiding the critical tasks will now be detrimental to the employee's financial situation – he or she has no better paying option in which to invest his or her efforts. Taking these steps motivates behavior that aligns with strategy, which is our goal.

Going back to our customer service call center example if the goal is to serve as many customers as possible quickly and efficiently then compensation should be tied to number of calls handled, average length of call or some similar measure. This may be most appropriate in an environment where the goal of each call is to simply schedule a repair visit. This should be handled quickly without any unnecessary fanfare.

If, on the other hand, our promise is to fully resolve customer issues on the first call then compensation should be tied some measure of successful issue resolution or a reduction of multiple customer contacts. In an environment where customer service reps are dealing with complex billing issues or tracking down lost shipments, solving problems may take more time and effort.

Thus it's not an issue of whether one measurement scheme is better than the other. Instead, the question to ask yourself is this:

Which measurement scheme drives the desired behaviors and supports the marketplace promise I've made?

As you move up through the organization, align upper management's compensation so that they only benefit when their subordinates best meet or exceed their targets. Even though management may be acting in a secondary or support role to the organization's operations, the compensation system is nonetheless must focus on results in support of strategy, just like with the frontline employees.

Monetary bonuses, in particular, serve as valuable tools to inspire workers to go beyond standard performance. Due to their importance, you will want to pay close attention to how they are structured.

A good structure will identify and compensate peak performers the most. An optimal system will drive creativity and also have contingencies for dealing with unique situations. The best systems drive those behaviors that are most consistent with the organization's chosen overarching strategy.

Again we challenge our clients to look for inconsistencies, conflicts and unintended consequences. Frontline employees should not have to choose between meeting the goals of Division A versus meeting the needs of Division B. Managers should not be rewarded when their subordinates miss their objectives. And nobody should be rewarded for behaviors that conflict with delivering the marketplace promise.

GROWTH OPPORTUNITIES

Along with financial incentives, another set of rewards act as very powerful motivators: access to growth opportunities.

Managers can provide excellent employees with any one or combination of the rewards listed below:

- Additional meeting time with management for the employee to discuss ideas or receive personalized constructive feedback
- Access to special or advanced training that may not be available or at least immediately available to others.
- Access to the employee's choice of projects/assignments or higher levels of responsibility on key projects.
- Recommendations for or support for promotions or transfers (when applicable).

Any one of these opportunities can assist in propelling an employee's career forward. By making them available to workers that execute the strategy, management sends a strong message about what it wants from its people.

HOW A SPOILED REWARD HINDERED SALES

When I was at Pillsbury (long before it was acquired by General Mills) I learned a valuable lesson about bonus structures and unintended consequences. This occurred while I worked on their crown jewel business – Refrigerated Dough. This is where the baking products that come in those little cans started and where the Pillsbury Doughboy originated. These dough products, like most refrigerated products, have a limited shelf life. Beyond a certain point, freshness is lost and the product must be removed from retail cases and tossed. To know when to toss product, the company utilized stamped on dates – the date when the product quality was no longer optimal. Demand was carefully forecast to move merchandise through the retail channel prior to reaching this date and minimize waste. As one might expect, throwing product in the dumpster can be a very expensive proposition.

Refrigerated Dough was a big moneymaker for the old Pillsbury Company. In fact, some employees often joked that we were a dough company with some interesting hobbies.

One of the biggest expense lines on the Refrigerated Dough P&L was the unsaleables. This was the charge taken for product that had become out-of-date and had to be destroyed. In the mid '90s, we were losing more than $20 million annually just on unsaleables.

Senior management believed that the root cause of this issue was based in sales, specifically how the sales force restocked the shelves. Salespeople were expected to rotate product in the stores by putting the close-dated product in front and the newer product toward the back of the displays. This ensured that the consumer grabbed the close-dated product first, thus removing potential future spoils from the shelf. (Please note again that products that had not reached their marked date were still fresh and just as good as the newer cans – Pillsbury never sold spoiled product!) The company was simply applying a FIFO (First In First Out) strategy for refrigerated product management at the shelf.

Management believed that the sales force was not rotating the product properly. After all, it was much easier to load a shelf from the front by pushing the close-dated product to the back than to load the shelf from the rear, keeping more recent product shipments in the front. To correct this perceived performance issue, management decided to reallocate part of the field sales bonus and tie it to a reduction in the amount of unsaleables. The targeted goal was to reduce unsaleables by 20 percent, resulting in a projected drop of $4 million of waste from the bottom line. Not bad.

On paper the new adjustment seemed ideal. Unfortunately, the creativity of the frontline sales staff to misuse the new system to their benefit was underestimated. Salespeople are wonderful at figuring out how to maximize rewards. It did not take them long to figure out that the easiest and most efficient method to drive down unsaleables from their perspective was to put less product on the store shelves. Less on-shelf inventory feeding constant demand meant fewer cans left on the shelf between each restocking. Of course this also meant that there were more out-of-stocks when the consumer went to the shelf to buy Pillsbury dough, but there was nothing in the reward structure that specifically demanded a balance between unsaleables and out-of-stocks. Put simply, the easiest way for the sales staff to accomplish a reduction in unsaleables and earn themselves the new bonus was to reduce overall product sales!

In the first three months of the bonus structure, total sales declined by 10 percent. Extrapolating those results, the total cost to the division in lost profit margin at that pace would exceed $40 million per year. Thus a simple alteration in the bonus structure designed to save the company $4 million annually would actually cost the company ten times that amount. Faced with this new reality, the compensation structure was quickly retooled to reward the sales force for reducing unsaleables while simultaneously maintaining the previous revenue levels.

WHAT CAN WE LEARN?

As we consider this story, three very important questions arise that are worth contemplating:

1) How would the delivery of Pillsbury's marketplace promise be enhanced by the reduction of unsaleables? Could it have resulted in purchases of old product (by leaving product on the shelf past the freshness date) and an unsatisfying customer experience? Were the customers (the retail stores and the overall consumers) better served by a shortage of product on the shelf? Might this have given competitors the opportunity to steal additional market share?

2) What aspects of the company's structure, culture, and rewards explicitly or implicitly communicated to the sales force that personal gain should take precedence over the customer and the financial stability of the organization? Surely such a significant reduction in revenue could have crippled or possibly caused the company to fail if it had been a new business or part of a fast growth industry.

3) What message is sent to employees in other parts of the company when this kind of story circulates? How can management counter the inevitable negative impact?

CONCLUSION

You have a lot to overcome internally in your organization to make employees effective. This is especially true when workers seem confused, or when divisions seem at odds with each other or, even worse, with what the customer expects. Despite the presence of these obstacles, you don't need to scrap the company and restart again. Instead, exploit the most important drivers to get everyone on the same page. Look at the culture you want (as determined by your unique strategy) and then communicate your path explicitly with ongoing messages and implicitly by aligning your actions to ensure consistency.

The first step is always to acknowledge that you need to proactively install a winning culture to support the execution of your strategy. Once you've made your marketplace promise, tell the organization that this is what matters most. Work to sell everyone on what the customers expect using a planned and methodical approach. Reinforce the message by developing and hiring talented people who can and will champion the strategy and by moving to a rewards system focused on paying for the fulfillment of customer expectations at key touchpoints within crucial processes. Taking these strategy-focused steps speaks volumes. Changing compensation and rewards goes a long way towards motivating the desired behaviors. The right people coupled with a well-designed rewards system can make your strategy work.

CHAPTER SEVEN

BUSINESS PROCESSES THAT DELIVER

"There is nothing so useless as doing efficiently that which should not be done at all."
—Peter Drucker

"Things which matter most must never be at the mercy of things which matter least."
—Goethe

INTRODUCTION

I was standing in the checkout line at my local Home Depot one day not long after they installed their new self-checkout lanes. I watched as a smiling clerk attempted to lure customers to the new technology and teach them how to check themselves out. She came over to the couple in front of me in line and suggested they try the new checkout process. Her selling pitch was interesting. She told the couple it would be faster and easier. Faster and easier for whom, I wondered? As she led them away to what I assumed was their maiden voyage through the new world of self checkout, the guy behind me looked at me with a scowl and remarked, *"If I wanted to be a checkout clerk at Home Depot, I would have applied for the job."*

I found his reaction very telling, not to mention refreshingly frank. Home Depot was trying to convince us that its new system was all about us (the customers). It was to make our experience faster and more convenient. To paraphrase Antonia (Don Quixote's niece) from *Man of La Mancha*, "They're only thinking of us!" Yet it's intuitively obvious to the most casual observer that this new feature is really all about Home Depot. While there are certainly times when the new checkout process *will* be more convenient for the customer, this change was clearly driven by the potential for real operating savings. The four-station self-checkout at Home Depot is managed by a single checkout clerk. With this new process, Home Depot has effectively transferred a portion of their labor expense back to the customer.

Is this a bad thing? I would argue that for companies like Home Depot, Wal-Mart, and Cub Foods, absolutely not. Why? Because their customer promise is low prices. That's why we, as customers, shop there. If we want somebody to pack our groceries and carry them to the car, we shop somewhere else, somewhere where the prices are higher and the company can afford to offer additional services. Rather than try to convince us that the new checkout process is for our "convenience," Home Depot should simply acknowledge that the new process allows them to keep prices low while fulfilling their promise: "You can do it. We can help."

Now imagine walking into Nordstrom, the Ritz Carlton, or Tiffany's and encountering a self-checkout lane. It doesn't work, does it? These are companies lauded for their commitment to personalized service. We pay a premium for that service and we would be appalled if we were asked to manage our own payment process.

The lesson here is that it's inappropriate to categorize a particular business process as inherently good or inherently bad. The process can only be judged in the context of your marketplace promise – the image you're trying to create in the marketplace. If your goal is to create a premium image and differentiate yourself from the competition by delivering world-class personalized service, then a self-serve checkout process doesn't align with your strategy. Thus, when we talk about business processes, we talk about the importance of designing and aligning your processes with the strategy you've chosen to pursue.

A process by general definition is a collection of steps performed in sequence that eventually result in a finished product or service. That product or service can be external for the marketplace or internal for other departments or functions. A well-designed process contains only those activities that are value-added, which means each individual task has worth to the ultimate recipient. To determine if a particular process is well-designed, you must shift your perspective from that of the organization or group performing the process to that of the end user (recipient).

To deliver a particular marketplace promise, you must always think of what customers value, not what the company traditionally does or wants to do. Customers have preconceived expectations about the quality, features, benefits, and timing tied to your product or service. These expectations were created by the promise you communicated. Your customers don't care how you manufacture or provide that outcome, only that it meets or exceeds their expectations. This point is so important it bears repeating: customers only care about the specific properties of the final product or service (and the related customer experience), not the specific methods of how your company achieved them.

When we talk about business processes, we will speak of three different types:

1) **Outward or Customer-Facing Processes:** These are processes that directly incorporate one or more primary customer touchpoints. They can be obvious, like selling processes (e.g. sales scripts, creating solutions, and

choosing products to pitch) or customer service processes (e.g. handling customer inquiries, ideas, or problems). They also include less obvious ones like billing statement delivery, customer segmentation (which ultimately determines how you approach the customer), credit reporting processes, and a host of others required to interact with customers and directly fulfill the marketplace promise.

2) **Horizontal Work-Flow Processes:** These are internal end-to-end business processes that support the organization's ability to perform crucial outward facing processes. Internal horizontal processes typically cross functional and divisional silo boundaries (e.g. order intake, order fulfillment, and product development). It's at the point of crossover that these processes generally break down. This failure most often occurs because it isn't clear who is in charge. The individual silo agendas have a tendency to overrule the overarching promise made to the marketplace. Alignment between what the customer expects and organizational capability becomes lost.

3) **Vertical Governance Processes:** These internal processes define how the organization is managed from top to bottom. They include the methods the CEO utilizes to lead and control his team to how the territory manager directs his sales representatives to how the plant manager supervises the line workers. The assumption is that if the senior staff is in alignment, then the folks doing the implementation across the organization are also aligned. Unfortunately, in many instances the objectives at the top are rarely heard as intended at the bottom, and the bigger the organization the less true alignment there is.

Most organizations possess about five to ten key (core) processes that drive their business, though the actual number for an individual organization varies depending on the range of markets served, the complexity of the offerings, and the amount of work that is done in-house. When we speak of these critical processes, we are speaking about large processes that cut broadly across organizational boundaries to deliver a finished product or service (usually to the marketplace customer). Larger processes will of course be composed of smaller subprocesses, some customer-facing and some that that work in the background. Most subprocesses are contained and maintained within a discreet functional or divisional silo. Successful businesses, however, thrive from the seamless operation of their holistic core processes as they move across the organization.

Some common core business processes are listed below:
- Strategic planning (including market assessment, analysis, and resource allocation)
- Client acquisition and retention (including marketing, selling, and customer service)
- Order fulfillment (including procurement of raw materials, scheduling, manufacturing, and shipping)
- Research and product development
- Information technology development and support

Different companies may define the limits of their processes in different ways, separating some into smaller categories and/or consolidating others into broader classifications. The point is that whatever you call or define as your key processes, your goal is to make them work together in one integrated system to most effectively and efficiently deliver your product or service to the final marketplace customer. Therefore, even though internal and governance processes may only deliver products to an internal end user (not typically the customer), ultimately that end user will take the result and apply it towards fulfilling some aspect of the customer promise.

MAPPING PROCESSES

Understanding and properly designing a business process requires that we must first map out (physically draw) the entire end-to-end sequence of activities. This exercise entails far more than simply generating a visual representation. The actual act of mapping out a process is something that will actively involve management across the organization in understanding the details of their inter-related operations.

This isn't one of those excruciatingly detailed process mapping exercises popularized by process re-engineering in the early 1990s. Those exercises ultimately focused on identifying and cutting out waste. As Kirsten Sandberg, an Executive Editor of *Harvard Business School Press*, noted in a recent article, in practice [1990s style] reengineering too often became a rationalization for downsizing staff, demoralizing employees, and ignoring corporate culture.

Process mapping for the purpose of aligning work-flow and decision-making to a marketplace strategy is far more simplistic. Experienced process wonks might even find it childish, but the beauty of this exercise is that it need not be complicated to be tremendously valuable. One of our clients discovered that they were losing valuable project time through excessive back-and-forth hand-offs between departments spread across multiple locations. By simply changing a few roles they streamlined the process. This cut weeks out of their time to market and increased the workload capacities of all departments involved. So with apologies to those who relish complexity, I present a short primer on process mapping for organizational alignment.

You may start with an existing business process for the purpose of analyzing how it currently performs, or you may wish to design a process from scratch to create an idealized map. Whichever method you use, the steps will essentially be the same; the differences arise in the questions you ask when undertaking the actual task of mapping.

Mapping a process can take up a lot of space and there are many different mediums on which the map can be drawn (e.g. paper, whiteboard, computer, or wall). Use whichever method you find convenient or simply just prefer. I will be describing a general procedure and you can tailor the details to accommodate your personal needs or preferences.

When we map a process, we are visually capturing all of the steps required (and which functional areas/departments perform them) to deliver a final product or service to an external marketplace customer (i.e. customer facing process) or to an internal customer/user (i.e. horizontal or vertical processes).

MAPPING AN EXISTING PROCESS

We'll begin with an example of an existing customer-facing process, in this case fulfilling a customer's order for product (please refer to figure 7.1 on next page).

First identify all the functional areas/departments that have a hand in processing the order. Write out these areas in the sequence they are encountered (as best you can) from left to right atop the sheet. Please note that I employ the leftmost column for listing the customer or end user, since they are the ultimate delivery point for a product or service and we want to easily see them. Next draw

Figure 7.1— Order Fulfillment Process Mapping

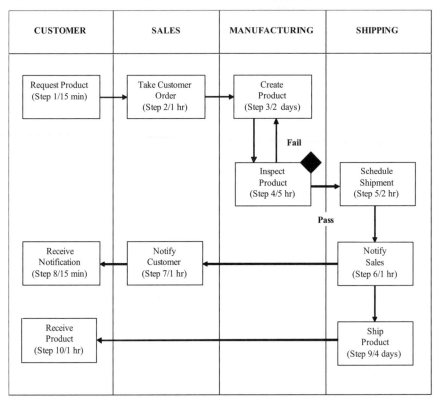

vertical lines down the page to separate the areas. Graphically, you are creating columns with the required functional areas as the headings for each column. Now, starting at the upper left corner (just below the first functional area column heading) draw a little square and inside that square write the first step that occurs in the order fulfillment process. In our example, the first column is for the customer and the first action is "*Request Product.*" Label this step with the number one and additionally add the time required for this step to occur. The next step falls under the vertical department of sales and is called "*Take Customer Order.*" Draw a box in that column with the action, label this step two, and add the time. Lastly, connect step one to step two using a directional arrow. Using this same approach, go through the entire existing process defining the actions under the appropriate functional area/department column, number the steps, and specify the required time to perform them. The finished product is a high-level map of the basic process.

There are many good resources to learn the more specific rules for drawing process flow maps, so I have not attempted to brief you on every little detail. However, there are a few simple conventions that you can follow to highlight important features and make the mapping easier to analyze:

- Start all process steps with an "action" verb since each step must accomplish something. (If you are not performing an action, how are you adding value?) The descriptive action you select should be an overall summary of what happens in the step, not a paragraph full of detailed description.

- Reorganize the vertical columns to more effectively show the proper process steps in sequence if necessary. (Mapping is sometimes an interactive process.)

- Number the steps in order. If you encounter a step that goes off in two or more directions (has two or more arrows going to other steps), just assign each diverging branch a letter and designate each successive step with both a number and letter (i.e. 3a, 4a, 5a vs. 3b, 4b, 4c).

- Place a symbol in decision steps to mark them as such (I use a black diamond in our example). These decision steps are where an approval or inspection may be required. If the process step passes, it moves to the next step in sequence; if the step fails, it may have to return to a prior step (loop back) to be repeated or the process may terminate. Label one arrow to the next step "*pass*" or "*yes*" and the loop back path "*fail*" or "*no*" to distinguish them.

You can take your map to the next level of detail using separate supplemental documentation if you wish. Use this additional documentation to write out Standard Operating Procedures (SOPs) showing individual tasks, who performs them (job role or function), and how much time is required to complete each one. Follow this procedure for every step on the process map. The overall process map allows upper-level management to get a high-level view of a process and ensures alignment across the silos to the overarching strategy. The SOPs provide specific lower-level details useful for the individuals actually responsible for carrying out a particular step.

Once you have a map, then thoughtful and effective analysis can begin. Note some of the following features evident on the process flow:

- Hand-offs (anywhere the process arrows cross the silos/ vertical lines).
- Bottlenecks (steps that require considerably larger amounts of time than other steps).
- Direct touchpoints with the customer (all boxes in the customer's column).
- Decision points (points where a product/service can move to the next step or be sent back for additional work).

Many times hand-offs result in long waiting times between steps because of poor communication between functional areas. Bottlenecks can occur because resources are not allocated effectively or because priorities differ between silos. Whatever the cause, effectiveness is hampered. Direct touchpoints are opportunities to serve the customer (you are directly interacting with them) and they affect the overall customer experience. Decision points let you know where potential rework is occurring. Keep these thoughts in mind as you ask yourself the following questions:

- Does each step add value by enhancing the quality, features, or benefits of the product/service, and more importantly, how does it align to our marketplace promise? If it does not, do I really need the step? If I need an unaligned step, how do I bring it into alignment with the strategy?

- How does each step affect the marketplace delivery of the product/service and the overall customers' experience (are there bottlenecks at some steps or miscommunications across boundaries that may negatively impact customers)?

- Is the number of customer (or end user) touchpoints appropriate (too few, too many)?

- How does each touchpoint add value that customers explicitly want? How are we turning each contact into an opportunity to better serve customers and show our commitment to our promise?

Ask yourself why the current conditions exist. Don't try to justify the situation; seek to understand the causes. Remember also when analyzing the steps not to fall into the trap of automatically assuming that an existing action is positive. For example, *Inspections* may on the surface appear to add value to a product (it reduces the chances of the customer getting a bad product), but improving the manufacturing process would serve the same objective. It would also speed up the delivery time by eliminating the need for inspection. Remember, from the customers' viewpoint, whether you inspected the product once, one hundred times, or if you simply had an error-free fabrication process ultimately doesn't matter; the customers simply want what they ordered in the condition promised.

MAPPING (DESIGNING) A NEW PROCESS

I mentioned previously that there is a difference when designing a process from scratch. There is. You start without any vertical functional areas. You begin with a completely blank page.

List out the specific level of quality, features, benefits, and the timing that you explicitly said you would provide the customer (or end user). Start brainstorming the steps of how to produce that product or service. Don't think of who performs the steps, just list out the actions that must be taken to make the final product or service contain the specific elements you listed. Put your steps into sequential order. This is the idealized process.

Start thinking about the capabilities of your organization. Where should the actions be performed and who should perform them? Create your vertical columns with the headings of the needed departments. You may find that some areas will need to be created or the steps outsourced. The objective here is to get away from thinking that specific functional areas or departmental roles have to be filled simply because they already exist in an organization. You want to focus on the customer promise and performing only those actions with your product or service that deliver that promise.

PROCESS STANDARDIZATION VS. PROCESS DIVERSITY

Larger organizations will need to make a decision between employing standard processes or diverse (or custom) processes across business units and divisions. Most large organizations today have grown through acquisition or by diversifying into whole new product and service areas. Like a mansion built wing by wing over the course of decades, each operating division tends to have its own style and its own way of doing things. Sometimes these differences create real customer value and competitive differentiation. Most of the time they don't. I wish I had a dollar for every general manager that has told me that his product or service is "different" and to conform his business processes to a corporate standard would be impossible.

Process Standardization: As the moniker implies, once you have designed the best way to fulfill orders, handle returns, analyze the market, etc., you uniformly apply that process across all business units, divisions, or products.

For example, suppose you had a very simple customer delivery process (for a product). The following steps are required to deliver the given order:

1) Confirm delivery date, time, and site with client.
2) Confirm directions with shipping.
3) Designate appropriate truck.
4) Load and fuel truck.
5) Deliver product the next morning.

Making this process standard means you would apply this methodology the same way throughout your organization, whether the order was for product x, y, or z, or whether it was for a customer in the Northeastern market or the Southwestern market.

Process Diversity (Custom Processes): Organizations customize processes (create special ones) when there are significant differences in their products or services or when the marketplace has very diverse characteristics that would not be properly served with a one size fits all approach. The primary advantage of employing a separate or modified process is that you are best able to leverage a product or customer segment opportunity that would be lost if treated the same as every other one.

The decision to customize a process should not be taken lightly. Two distinct disadvantages accompany the use of custom processes:

they require additional management time or resources to oversee them, and there are extra costs for differentiated training, tools, and communications.

The choice between which approach to take is purely dependent upon the unique position of the organization. Companies can mix the two approaches, taking advantage of the efficiency of standardized processes where applicable and using diverse processes where it economically makes sense to deliver a particular product/service or satisfy the needs of a particular customer segment. The key, however, is making a conscious choice based on the true needs of the marketplace. Too often, independent-minded division general managers will drive a company toward unnecessarily customized processes. They are well-intentioned, but the end result can be a hodgepodge of customer experiences that don't align with the expectations created by the overall promise.

SIMULATION

Maybe you think you have perfected your processes at this point. There is only one sure way to know. Whether analyzing an existing process or creating a new one, it is essential you understand how the process ultimately delivers to the customer. How do you do this? You accomplish it through simple simulation techniques. All it takes is a little imagination, a willingness to adopt the customer's perspective (by asking difficult questions), and your completed process maps.

Business has been around for a very long time; the typical situations you will encounter with customers (the kind that make up about 99 percent of your encounters) can be anticipated ahead of time. So go ahead and plan in advance, apply these typical encounters to your processes, and see what the outcome reveals. This exercise should be conducted twice: first from the customer's point of view to "feel" the customer's experience, and then a second time internally from the management and employee point of view to see why customers experience the process as they do. As you make process changes over time and refine different steps, you will naturally want to repeat the entire exercise.

Note: As we continue this discussion, I will typically refer to the customer as the beneficiary of a process's final results. When faced with analyzing horizontal or vertical workflows just substitute "end user" for the customer. The same conditions will apply even though end users don't pay with money; they have needs that must be met to achieve smooth business operations. Regardless of whether the final customer (end user) is external or internal, you still want to get the transaction right.

CUSTOMER VIEWPOINT SIMULATION

For each process, take a look at what the customer (or end user) expects of the product or service. Again, these expectations must be driven by the overall marketplace promise. A promise of everyday low prices yields a very different set of expectations than a promise of pampered luxury. Now pretend you are the customer and you wish to purchase your product or service. Analyze the following elements common to almost all business transactions:

- What is my experience with the ordering process (easy, difficult, lacking information or answers to questions)?
- Does the company know my wants/needs for quality, features, benefits, and timing (how does it know)?
- How is the actual timing of the product or service (too long, too short, just right)?

- Does the final product meet my actual wants/needs for quality, features, and benefits?
- How am I kept informed about the status of my order?
- How am I contacted or informed of changes or potential problems (affecting delivery, availability, options)?
- How am I compensated if there are changes or problems on the company's part (am I happy with the level of compensation)?
- If I have changes or problems initiated from my side, how can I contact the company (is this communication easy, hard, impossible)?
- How is my product or service delivered (is this acceptable given the amount of time and money I have invested with the company)?
- How are regular or standard returns handled (easy, difficult, not accepted)?
- How am I billed (or my account(s) tracked)?
- How can I communicate a problem with my bill or my account (is this easy, hard, impossible)?
- Is after-sales service provided and how is it accessed (is this easy, hard, impossible)?
- How can I provide general feedback on my experience to the company?

Does your process address these items in a way that matches the image you wish to cultivate in the marketplace? If not, what's out of alignment and how would customers perceive your organization at this point in the process? What steps in the process are missing or causing problems? How do we fix them?

Most likely, simulating the customer experience as you go through the process will lead to some modifications to streamline a process to include only actions that the customer perceives as having worth. You will also want to add any steps to address common transactional occurrences that are not presently accounted for. When you finally get to the process you feel most effectively and efficiently meets the customer expectations, it is time to look at it from an internal organizational perspective. This step is taken to ensure that the organization itself is not structured in a way that makes performing the process difficult.

INTERNAL VIEWPOINT SIMULATION

Once again, look at the end-to-end process. This time, however, assume the role of a frontline worker or manager. In this role, ask the following two questions at each step:

- What internal organizational mechanisms (training, tools, compensation, internal communications) reinforce this step being performed as the company optimally envisions it?
- What internal organizational mechanisms (training, tools, compensation, internal communications) hinder this step?

An experience with my local phone company illustrates this challenge. I had two phone lines coming into my house. At some point, to make life easier, I consolidated both numbers onto a single monthly bill. Eventually, I found it necessary to split the two numbers back out into separate bills. This seemed like an easy task. After all, I remember consolidating the numbers onto one bill required only a simple phone call. How difficult could it be to reverse that process?

I called my phone company's customer service number to make my request. The customer service representative was extremely nice and said she would be happy to make that happen. However, as she started to move through the transaction I could feel her frustration rising. She finally informed me that "the system would not allow her to enter the request."

She asked me to hold while she consulted her manager.

Five minutes later I was informed that while this seemed like a simple request nobody in the department knew how to make the system comply.

I actually felt sorry for the representative that fielded my call. She sincerely wanted to solve my problem. But the tools she was given hindered her ability to make what appeared to be a simple billing change.

Does your organization's infrastructure reinforce or hinder the performance at each step? (Remember now, you are looking at a process with steps you've determined the customer wants.) It makes no sense to have the perfect process if the organization trains, rewards, and communicates a different direction or does not have the right tools to perform the work. Take the following actions:

- Make sure the organization as a whole knows the steps involved in the key processes (establish a place where the source maps and details of processes (SOPs) reside and are accessible to employees that work on them).

- Ensure communications don't provide conflicting information or messages about the process's steps

- Monitor training to ensure that the knowledge, skills, and abilities being fostered apply to performing the steps of the processes employees actually work at (make sure trainers understand the processes under their scope as well).

- Give employees the right tools for the job at each step.

- Adjust employee compensation to give incentive for people to do those tasks that the process requires to operate optimally (update employee objectives as processes are updated).

- Compensate process managers for the successful delivery of a process outcome, not individual metrics.

You know what customers are expecting (your marketplace promise), so use that information to ask your organization how well your processes can deliver on that promise. Anticipate foreseeable problems and fix them or plan to provide acceptable options before your customers even have to ask. Then make sure your employees perform their processes as intended by reinforcing the strategy with matching internal systems and structures.

INTEGRATING A PROCESS MANAGEMENT STRUCTURE

We have talked a lot about the details of business processes and how to map them out and then analyze them from the customer and internal perspectives. It is also important to understand how to effectively implement and maintain a process internally so that it doesn't stray from the company's overall strategy or marketplace promise. As I've pointed out, the subprocesses of each core business process will still reside in individual silos, and the tendency for managers to "improve" their small piece without consideration of the bigger process picture is always a danger. Keeping core business processes on track requires a different managerial style and control system from one that emphasizes goals set by individual functions or units operating in a stand-alone capacity.

THE CURRENT SILO MANAGEMENT STYLE

Typically, managers that have progressed through their careers in organizations that have strong silos are accustomed to a command and control style to lead their people. They have had little reason to cooperate across boundaries in the past and may not possess the necessary skills to do so in the present. They may not fully understand the entire core process or their role in the overarching workflow chain and may believe that only they can determine the best way to process work through their particular area. Finally, as with any organizational change initiative, when people have built their career with an organization and are then told a new process is being installed, these long-time employees may feel that embracing the new process means admitting everything they accomplished up to this point was not good enough. Why else is a change needed at this time? All of these elements can lead to some managers being unprepared for, resisting, or even undermining the execution of the new processes that focus on the marketplace strategy.

To illustrate how this problem originates, consider the product development and commercialization process. The individual silos (vertical columns) may include R&D, Procurement, Operations, Marketing, etc. Imagine you are an R&D manager who for years has only had to worry about those steps residing in your particular silo. You are rewarded for product innovation and design. You've built a high-performing, creative team of engineers who have distinguished themselves time and time again. You have monitored and controlled your output by applying metrics and policies that drive innovation and out-of-the-box thinking. But your team has worked in isolation or near isolation. You may have had some minimal interaction with the areas on either side of your silo, but it has not been a priority. In fact you believe that sheltering your team from the rest of the organization allows the creative process to flourish. The company's compensation system has always rewarded you only for your area's work results. You have little or no incentive to collaborate with other managers outside your domain. You run a tight ship and are rewarded appropriately for doing so.

Now the market shifts. Customers change. Lower prices become the dominant need in the marketplace surpassing product features and innovation. But your department's relative isolation has desensitized them to cost issues. It's unclear how your designs affect downstream departments. Some of your innovations could result in hard cost increases by driving decreases in manufacturing throughput or adding new inventories of unique raw materials. Some may result in soft cost increases by adding new vendors to Procurement's workload. These cost increases drive prices up and could make the company uncompetitive, offering product features the market no longer wants at a price it is no longer willing to pay.

Unfortunately, if every silo in the company remains independent or is only concerned about their immediate neighbors, the entire system (process) as a whole is not assured of working optimally. The methods or timing of output of steps at the beginning of the process may negatively impact critical steps much further down the line. However, since coordination between silos is not happening (or in a very limited capacity), problems or even opportunities cannot be easily seen. There is no designated person with responsibility for identifying potential overarching problems or improvement opportunities.

A NEW APPROACH TO PROCESS MANAGEMENT

It requires a lot of time and effort to change a culture, align processes and systems with strategy, and to learn to consistently stay focused and deliver the promise. The organization needs to rise above its silos and manage its core processes holistically if true strategy alignment is to be achieved. I would be remiss in having you think I could simply provide a blueprint for accomplishing that task in a few brief paragraphs and your organization would then enthusiastically follow the plan. That said, below I provide some general overview actions that will lay the foundation and move you toward consistent execution of your marketplace promise.

1) **Carefully select senior managers to serve as process owners to oversee your critical processes end-to-end.** The individuals you choose need to remain in these positions (not serve as temporary project managers) to create long-term accountability for proper delivery, act as a resource of knowledge, and serve as a guide as each core process evolves. These managers must clearly exhibit the ability to influence, negotiate, and coach since they will be working with silo managers as well as frontline individuals to achieve process goals. They must have a great comfort level with collaborative team approaches and rely less on hierarchical or bureaucratic governing structures. Give these process owners the authority to set their own process metrics and hold workers accountable for reaching them. The manager's compensation itself should be based on metrics measuring the processes' performance as a whole rather than meeting numbers for individual steps or specific functional/departmental areas internal to the process.

2) **Process owners must play a continual part in remapping their processes as time and marketplace factors demand changes.** They are responsible for ensuring that after subsequent changes each step still aligns to the overall marketplace promise. They also need to continually assess the metrics and make any required adjustments or generate whole new metrics as dictated by alterations to the process.

3) **Once people know what you want them to do, give them the ability to do it properly. Match the proper tools to the job (not the other way around).** Giving people the

necessary equipment and proper training also sends an implicit message: be successful. We'll discuss tools further in *Chapter 8*.

4) **Start aligning recruitment, training, and compensation to reinforce the strategy. Put out communications showing how the business processes match with and drive delivery of the organizational strategy.** As we've learned from looking at an organization's culture, it's what you do that sends the loudest message. When management changes the supporting internal systems to align with the processes that deliver the over-arching customer promise, it removes conflicting behavior.

5) **Make continuous analysis and improvement if its processes a priority.** New and better methods will always be developed, and when they are the right fit, they need to be incorporated. Examining processes on a continual basis also helps to maintain the discipline of focusing on customers' needs and wants (a very good thing for any ongoing business). Simulate your customers' experiences to see how they perceive the organization. Adopt the perspective of management frontline workers to determine why they might be inclined to deviate from strategy. Work consistently to remove obstacles and provide the work force with the best path to meet the customers' expectations.

A TALE OF TWO RETAILERS

Processes that directly touch customers should be given extra attention to ensure that they are well thought out, understood, and monitored by management to meet the expectations of those customers. Remember, the customer's experience will define your organization in the marketplace. In the following examples, I show

how a simple thing like a retailer's product return process can either win a customer for life or drive one away forever.

COSTLYTOYZ – A COMMITMENT TO EXCELLENCE?

As a typical consumer, I recently purchased a new alarm clock radio from one of my favorite gadget stores, CostlyToyz (clearly a ficticious name devised to conceal the true identity of the proprietor). The alarm clock is CostlyToyz branded as is much of their unique and exclusive merchandise. I was impressed by the clock's packaging, which authoritatively stated, *"We improve your life through innovative products and our unwavering commitment to excellence."* Now that is quite a marketplace promise!

The clock's features included the ability to set the time itself, keep track of up to twenty radio stations, and wake up the user with his or her choice of either music or an alarm buzzer. The setup instructions were fairly straightforward. I excitedly plugged in my new clock and as promised, it instantly set itself to the correct time. Very impressive! Within mere minutes I had set three of the presets to my favorite radio stations, tested the alarm, and then set it to wake me at 6:00 a.m. the following day.

At 6:15 a.m. the next morning I awoke to the unpleasant sound of static blaring from my new toy. Perplexed, I tried all the presets that had been set the night before, but sadly received only more static. I turned off the radio and noticed that the alarm light that was lit the previous night to indicate the clock alarm was set no longer seemed to work. Hoping to "reboot," I unplugged the unit and replugged it back in, but nothing seemed to work. I could no longer set the alarm or tune in a single radio station. Clearly my clock was defective.

I was sure that CostlyToyz would replace the item, so I didn't let myself get too bent out of shape over the situation. I simply plugged my old alarm clock back in and went about my day. It took me almost a week to get back to the mall where I had purchased the product. Even so, I confidently entered the store carrying the carefully reboxed product and proceeded to the desk where a sales clerk politely asked me how he could help. I told him I had purchased the clock radio six days prior at that particular store and that I needed to exchange it for a working model. The clerk responded by saying he would get the manager.

The manager emerged from the back of the store and promptly asked what my problem was. His choice of the word "problem" struck me as overly presumptive. I told him there wasn't any problem, that I had simply purchased a clock radio that was apparently defective and that I would like to have it replaced. He asked if I had my receipt. I looked in the bag, but didn't find it. When I stated as much to the manager, he informed me that he could not make the exchange without the receipt. My response went something along the lines of, "Sure you can. This is clearly CostlyToyz merchandise – it says so right on the box. It doesn't work. I do not want a refund. I would just like you to give me another one and send this defective one back to the factory." The manager then uttered those annoying words that have become infamous in the annals of American retailing: "I'm sorry sir; we can't process a return without a receipt. **That's our policy.**"

I was stunned. I didn't want to "process a return." I just wanted to make an exchange for a product that worked. I asked him if it was also CostlyToyz's **policy** not to stand behind merchandise that carries its name. He merely repeated, "Our policy clearly states that we can't process a return without a receipt." I realized that I was essentially dealing with an automaton that had little authority to solve my problem and that to further engage him would be pointless. Still, I had to ask, "Does it bother you that you've just lost a customer for life?" He simply shrugged. I walked out carrying my carefully repackaged, non-working clock radio and the impression that CostlyToyz's *unwavering commitment to excellence* extends only to those customers who remember to save their receipts.

Let's compare this experience to an experience I had last year at Nordstrom.

NORDSTROM – LEGENDARY CUSTOMER SERVICE

Its pretty well documented that Nordstrom provides legendary customer service. Here's a personal experience I had with them that proves that point once again.

During the holidays last year I received a beautiful sweater from my parents who live in New York. Knowing that I had recently lost a significant amount of weight, they were unsure of my size, so they purchased the sweater at their local Nordstrom. Doing so ensured that if they purchased the wrong size, I would be able to exchange it at my Nordstrom here in Minnesota. That was a good plan except for the fact that Nordstrom tailors its stock to local tastes, and that what is available in its New York stores isn't necessarily available in its Minnesota stores.

Sure enough the sweater was too big. Way too big. It needed to be exchanged. I didn't have a receipt, not even a gift receipt. All I had was the little Nordstrom price tag still attached to the garment, ripped in half, lest I know how much my parents paid for my gift.

Still, I walked into the men's department at the local Nordstrom, presented my sweater to the sales clerk, and asked if I could exchange it for a smaller size. Her first response was, "I'm sorry sir, that's not a Nordstrom product. We don't carry that brand of sweater in our department." I was impressed that she had such a confident knowledge of her product line. I pointed out the ripped Nordstrom tag on the garment, which surprised her. She picked up her bar code scanner and tapped the still intact code on the tag. Instantly her computer displayed the item. She apologized and explained that this particular item was only sold in their Northeast stores.

At this point I assumed I wasn't going to be able to exchange the item for another size unless I was prepared to hop a plane to La Guardia. Did I have any other options? The sales clerk politely offered me two: I could either return the item right there for a cash refund, or she would order a smaller size from a New York store and have it delivered to my home. Considering I still wasn't sure what the right size was, I took the cash.

Nordstrom promises complete customer satisfaction, and even in less than optimal circumstances I walked out a very satisfied customer.

COMPARING THE TWO EXPERIENCES

Perhaps it's unfair to compare a CostlyToyz customer experience to a Nordstrom customer experience. Nordstrom's dogged pursuit of world class customer service is well known. They have aligned their people, processes and tools to this single-minded pursuit. In the example above, there was no return policy blocking the clerk's action. She had sole discretion to make the return decision. She also had a tool, an inventory system that tracked products sold throughout the Nordstrom chain, which gave her the necessary information to make an informed decision. Nordstrom has just one guiding principle – "When it comes to customers, use your best judgment." That's the process the company determined best enabled delivery of its marketplace strategy.

Still, CostlyToyz opened itself up to scrutiny by promising to enhance the quality of my life through its "*innovative products and unwavering commitment to excellence*" pledge and then not fulfilling that promise. To be fair to CostlyToyz, however, this example was just one story about one store in a whole chain. I have no idea if CostlyToyz really has such an unyielding return policy or if this occasion was merely an isolated management training issue. I do know that in today's harsh competitive environment, it only takes one bad experience to lose a customer for life.

What can we learn about process alignment from these examples? Consider for a moment the common but critical process of providing customer service for returning merchandise in the context of a company's desired marketplace image. A thorough review of said company's return process map should involve answering the questions shown below:

1) Has the company analyzed its return process from a customer viewpoint recognizing there are many different causes that drive returns?

2) Does the return policy logically and adequately accommodate each potential return scenario to the customer's satisfaction? (Remember, the customers don't care about the policy, they care about being treated appropriately.)

3) Given the application of the policy to each particular situation, does the resulting level of customer satisfaction match the image and marketplace promise the organization wants to present?

4) What are the economic advantages and disadvantages of giving store managers discretion in interpreting the return

policy and how do these fit with the company's business model? What changes need to be made to training, communications, and accountability for store managers in the event the company chooses to upgrade their authority levels?

5) In the case of CostlyToyz, if the organization actually has a more liberal return process but managers are ignoring it, could there be a systemic cultural or financial reason? Perhaps the compensation structure does not support the process (i.e. managers take a hit to their P&L for returns received).

6) Would both the company and its customers be better served if the company considered the lifetime profitability of satisfied customers rather than focusing on individual transactions? (A single transaction may cost the company money but ultimately maintain an ongoing profitable customer relationship.)

CONCLUSION

Once you make promises to the customers in the marketplace, you need operations to back up your statements. Understand the capability of your organization by understanding your key processes. Map them out and analyze them. Make sure the work you are doing is delivering on the promise and don't be confined by artificial departmental boundaries. Silos do not serve customers, the right processes do. That's why you need to make sure your organization's culture and communications support complete end-to-end processes and the overarching customer experience.

Once you've given your managers and frontline employees direction, give them responsibility and accountability for their processes. Go back and simulate the "customer" viewpoint; run through and test your processes to determine how they deliver on common business scenarios, handle potential problems, and capitalize on opportunities. Ask yourself how each step in a process supports the delivery of your marketplace promise, differentiates you from the competition, and builds the reputation you seek. Keep pushing and refining your processes and your customers – as well as your bottom line – will benefit.

CHAPTER EIGHT

THE RIGHT TOOL FOR THE JOB

"Never underestimate the power of a simple tool."
– Craig Bruce

"But technology is a tool, not a virtue."
– Emily G. Balch

INTRODUCTION

A while back I received a call from a longtime client about a potential new project. He informed me that his division's "marketing message" had lost its effectiveness in the previous twelve months and a new message was needed. In essence, what he was saying was that he needed a new marketplace promise because the old promise was no longer compelling.

In my experience, marketplace promises, if well-conceived, don't work one day and then just stop working the next. Certainly markets shift, customers' needs change, and new competitors arise with better offerings, but these changes tend to gradually reduce the effectiveness of a promise. To observe that a promise has stopped working over a twelve month period is unusual.

Somewhat skeptical, I started probing. I inquired about what had convinced my client that his marketing message was no longer effective. What measurement was he using to arrive at this conclusion? He explained that his marketing efforts, mostly direct mail, were designed to drive leads to the sales organization. Most of these leads came in by phone or via the Internet. The leads were captured in a centralized leads distribution database and then parceled out to the individual salespeople based on geography, workload, and sales expertise. The process utilized was fairly sophisticated. Each lead was tracked through the system until a salesperson either closed the sale or closed the lead. Sales personnel entered details regarding the ultimate disposition of each lead so that marketing could then analyze the number of leads hitting the sales force and also the customer objections that limited sales.

So the total number of leads was measured at the end of the process and actually served as a gauge of leads dispositioned by sales (rather than total leads generated and consolidated in the centralized system). On the surface, this measure appeared to make sense. A lead has no value if it isn't acted upon; measuring lead activity is a solid organizational measure. However, is it the right measure to determine the effectiveness of a marketing strategy?

My client told me that the number of leads dispositioned in the past twelve months was half of those dispositioned in each of the past three years. So my client's promise was driving a consistent level of inquiries for three solid years and then all of the sudden it stopped working? My alarm bells were ringing big time. I told him that before we embarked on a project to retool the message that I would like to spend some time tracing the leads distribution process. We did just that.

What we found was quite enlightening. The number of leads *generated* and captured by the centralized system actually *increased* over the past year. Unfortunately, this wasn't a measure easily calculated and took some real data sleuthing on our part.

However, a simple programming change in an unrelated sales system unintentionally broke the lead distribution system. As a result, only about half the leads transmitted by the centralized server ever made it to their intended field sales recipients. The others were being lost in cyberspace. Thus, the result was that the number of leads dispositioned by the field decreased by 50 percent versus one year ago. What makes this story even more intriguing is that the system change that ultimately led to the loss of the lead distribution functionality was actually driven by the operations group. Operations had absolutely no idea that the system change it implemented would have an effect on an unrelated sales system.

I tell this story as a prime example of the importance of tools to the implementation of strategy. We could have spent months reworking the client's marketing message, but the results would have probably been the same or worse. The problem wasn't the message, and it wasn't the promises being made. The problem was a broken tool deep inside the internal system of the organization. In response, the project quickly shifted from strategy creation to infrastructure repair.

When marketplace results fall short of our expectations, we are too quick to blame the strategy. As we said in the front of the book, when a strategy fails, it's rarely the strategy itself that is at fault, but the execution of that strategy that is too blame. The wrong people, the wrong culture, bad processes, and inadequate tools all play a role in marketplace failure.

In *Chapter 6* we said that businesses rely on their people to deliver the marketplace promise to the customer. In *Chapter 7* we said that these employees are guided by the general business processes that manage workflow across the organization and out to the customer. In this chapter, we will recognize that our people rely on the tools we give them to accomplish their work in the most efficient and effective manner possible. Business tools come in all shapes and sizes and exhibit a variety of characteristics. Fortunately, though, we can compress their wide range of variability into three useful tool groupings that are shown below:

- ***Task Tools:*** Enable the completion of a specific task (tasks are actions that comprise the individual steps in a process).

- ***Information Tools:*** Provide information necessary to do one's job.

- ***Communication Tools:*** Enable communication between individuals (either internally along the steps of a process or externally with customers).

Each of these tool categories enables a business process to be completed. Of course, just as your people and your processes must be in alignment with the organizational strategy, the tools a company utilizes must also be in alignment with that overall strategy and enable that strategy's implementation in the marketplace.

If, for example, our promise is to be *"Like a Good Neighbor,"* but when a customer calls we don't know who they are because our representative answering the phone can't quickly access customer information and identify to whom they are speaking, how good of a neighbor are we? In this example, we have not equipped our customer service staff with a tool that enables them to live up to our commitment. We need to ensure that we drive the strategy of *"Like a Good Neighbor"* through not just our choice of advertising & brochures to communicate the promise but also, and just as importantly, by making sure the organization has all of the tools necessary to fulfill that promise when interacting with customers and handling their requests.

The meaning of that approach is simply applying information tools that make customers feel like we know whom they are when calling. It includes human communication tools as opposed to voice recognition menus. (Could you imagine meeting your neighbor over the fence and the first thing he says to you is, "To gossip about Pete's wife press or say one, to comment on the weather press or say two…"?) Finally, we must include task tools that enable the customer representative to perform the tasks that instantly solve the customers' problems, whether it requires fixing a billing error, adding coverage, or just answering a simple question. That's what good neighbors do.

From personal experience, it seems every time I call a company these days I get a recording that asks me to identify myself by entering personal information (e.g. SSN, phone number) or an account number. I am told that this is so the company can properly route my call. Then I am asked a series of questions to identify why I'm calling. Yet when I finally get to a customer representative, that individual neither knows who I am or the reason why I'm calling, which means I have to go through the whole process again. So why did I have to enter all that information into the phone in the first place? When customers see a company using inappropriate tools or wrongly applying them, it results in a frustrating customer experience and diminishes their confidence (and rightly so) in the organization's ability to deliver on its promises.

BUSINESS OVER COFFEE

Let's look at the example of the simple coffee shop. I happen to frequent many different shops – Caribou, Starbuck's, Dunn Brothers, and some independents. It all depends on where I am and where I have to be when the caffeine craving strikes. On one morning in particular, I just happened to be in my favorite shop, Caribou. As I placed my order, I carefully observed the tools the staff used to sell and serve me a cup of coffee. It started at the cash register when I gave my drink order. The cash register is multifunctional and actually incorporates all three tool types. First it enables the *tasks* of both counting and storing my money. It provides *information* to the cashier regarding how much change to return and it provides *information* to accounting about how much money was collected during the shift. It also *communicates* my order to a little touch screen over by the barista. This screen is a tool for keeping track of orders. The screen is strictly a *communication* tool. It communicates to the barista what drink to make. When the drink is completed, the barista touches the order on the screen and it disappears. To make the drink itself, the barista uses an espresso machine. This machine is a *task* tool. It doesn't communicate or provide information. It just brews coffee. Of course, it's also the most important tool in the process, because without it, I don't get my coffee.

The choice of tools affects the overall customer experience at the coffee shop, the complexity of the operation, and the fulfillment of the marketplace promise. I've noticed that my other coffee spots don't necessarily use the same tools. For example, instead of a fancy touch screen to communicate my order, some shops just write a special code on the cup. The touch screen is the high-tech option; the pen is the low-tech option. Both tools enable the process of communicating my order to the barista.

I've further noticed at some of my coffee spots that the barista must personally go through the process of grinding my beans and loading the grounds into a receptacle, which is then manually attached to the espresso machine. While that's all very authentic, it can be tedious when I'm late for a meeting. Caribou stores, conversely, have chosen to use an automatic brewing system. The espresso machine grinds the beans, loads itself, and brews the coffee, all in about half the time it takes the other shops performing these steps manually. When you're waiting for that first cup of the day, those saved seconds can be an eternity. The automatic machine also ensures that there is less variability in the process at Caribou. The machine measures and loads the exact amount of grounds the same way every time. I don't have to worry about a confused trainee or a sleepy-eyed barista shorting me on my caffeine.

The coffee story is my way of showing that we can choose different types of tools to enable our business processes and ultimately deliver a unique promise in the marketplace. The choice of tools needs to align with our organizational strategy – that is, with the customer experience we wish to drive. My local independent coffee house wants to maintain its anti-corporate, anti-establishment image and deliver an individualized customer experience. For this business, marking cups with ink and personally grinding beans adds to the experience it's selling. It is irrelevant that the process takes a little longer, because its customers aren't in that much of hurry. Caribou, on the other hand, clearly got direction from its customers that speed and consistency were more important than an individualized experience, so it adjusted its process and acquired tools to deliver the fast, consistent experience its customers crave. It would be inappropriate to say one set of tools is superior to the other. It's only important that the tools you choose enable you to deliver the experience you've promised.

THE RIGHT TOOL FOR THE JOB

There are some great historical examples out there of companies that really understood the opportunity to match the right tools to the job. They succeeded in setting new standards for whole business categories by choosing and/or developing tools that enabled them to create *and* execute their unique marketplace strategies.

Jiffy Lube® pioneered the fast oil change industry in 1979 by developing the first drive-through service bay. This special bay enabled the company to provide customers with rapid and professional maintenance service for their vehicles. The bay and the manner in which it was equipped gave the service technicians the ability to provide an express oil change more quickly than the previous standard. Jiffy Lube didn't stop there. It is responsible for some of the major advances in automotive preventive maintenance service, including the now ubiquitous window cling reminder sticker that helps drivers keep track of their oil change intervals. This simple tool communicated to Jiffy Lube customers when it was time for an oil change and kept them coming back at regular intervals.

Another example is LensCrafters, which emerged in 1983 and was the first optical retailer to promise the delivery of prescription eye glasses in about an hour. The company consolidated the eye doctor, optical laboratory, and a wide selection of frames under one roof to provide its customers with a convenient and complete optical shopping experience. Lots of other retail stores sold frames at the time, but LensCrafters put the tools necessary for enabling the task of grinding lenses right in the stores. This choice of placement for its tools was what enabled it to promise glasses in an hour and consistently fulfill that promise. It also strongly differentiated LensCrafters from every other competitor in the optical marketplace.

Finally, Wal-Mart was utilizing computers to link its stores and warehouses by the 1970s. Through tracking sales data and intelligently applying this information to coordinate delivery schedules,

Wal-Mart was able to track specific products and thereby reduce potential inventory miscalculations. Wal-Mart targeted a low-cost business strategy and supported it very effectively by utilizing information technology tools to increase efficiency and eliminate waste in its distribution model.

Businesses thrive when they tap into the wants and needs of the market and don't disappoint in the delivery. Look at the tools your organization is using. Do they provide your people with the ability to satisfy your customers' expectations the way these example organizations have?

TASK TOOLS

Task tools are designed to perform a specific work task. By necessity they come in all variety of shapes, sizes and functions. Some common examples are listed below:

- Manufacturing machinery (e.g. mixers, fillers, robotic arms, carton sealers)
- Construction machinery (e.g. welders, concrete mixers)
- Office tools (e.g. staplers, paper clips, calculators, computers)

This seems to be the one tool category that companies most often get right. Tasks are very tangible subparts of a process step. It's easy to identify their inputs and relatively easy to define the desired outputs. Beans in, consistently brewed, awesome tasting coffee out. Glass in the grinder, eyeglass lenses out. The only trick is to ensure you really understand what the desired output is (as defined by the customer) and acquire the right tools to enable that outcome.

If you are the coffee shop manager, does your customer want consistent coffee prepared fast or a personally brewed cup made with tender loving care? You need to know which grinding machine to purchase and the amount of training required. It all comes back to following your strategy and remembering your promises and the customer expectations they create.

If you have aligned your organization's marketplace strategy and supplied business processes that support this objective, then you should have a thorough understanding of what needs to occur within each step of your processes. Go back down to the specific experience elements for the tasks that comprise a process step. Identify the most appropriate tools to satisfy them specifically. Caution: don't try to fix bad processes with better tools. If you do not have the proper alignment, your people will inevitably be performing non-value added work despite how new or good the tools they have been given are. Get the process aligned to the strategy first, drill down to the proper steps, tasks, and the experience elements that must be satisfied, and then make the choice of tools.

Even the simple task of digging a ditch requires the proper tool. Digging ditches is a fairly straightforward task. Shovel the dirt and create a trench. But should you use a manual shovel or a sophisticated backhoe? We assume that if we upgrade a ditch digger's shovel to a backhoe, we will get increased productivity. Seems easy, the employee can now move more dirt. However, if the employee isn't skilled in the use of the backhoe, any potential performance increases enabled by the new and more powerful tool will likely be lost because of a lack of competency. Worse yet, some real property damage or injury could result. Additionally, what if the customers you serve only want narrow, shallow ditches because of buried piping and electrical lines? That backhoe lacks the necessary precision and no longer looks like such a good investment. In this case, a simple shovel in the hands of a careful laborer would be a better option. Always ask if you are using the right tool for what the customer requires and ensure that the tool's operators understand what the desired outcome is.

INFORMATION TOOLS

One of the biggest issues plaguing business today is an overabundance of data and very little useful information. We call this scenario data rich, information poor. The technology in place to capture data has in some cases outstripped our ability to analyze that data and draw meaningful, actionable conclusions from it. Information tools have firmly integrated themselves into everyday business processes and are an integral part of customer-facing processes.

Think about a grocery chain with one thousand stores. The checkout scanners record every single purchase of every single customer every single day. If each store averages 100 customers per hour that are buying ten items each, that's 1 million data points captured every hour! In just three months that number easily tops 1 billion individual sales. These sales are actually spread out across some 30,000 to 50,000 grocery items the chain carries. How can the chain sort through this mountain of raw data to drive stocking decisions? Analytical tools are required to separate fast-moving items from slower items, high margin-items from low-margin items, regional items driven by regional tastes and traffic drivers (i.e. milk) from impulse items (i.e. decadent chocolate chip cookies), and so on.

We use the word *information* to clearly distinguish meaningful numbers, trends, and patterns from simple raw data. The creation of this information requires several types of tools. First there are *data collection* tools. The checkout scanner is a data collection tool. Next there are the *data storage* tools. Checkout scanner data from each store is typically transmitted to some type of central database, aggregated, and held for later use. Finally there are the *analytical tools*. These tools access the raw data in storage and manipulate it to create information ultimately serving as business insights. Some analytical tools may be as simple as a personal computer database query tool that is linked to spreadsheet software. Other tools can be as sophisticated as automated monitoring algorithms that require little human intervention.

Now, I've cast my examples in terms of technology, such as scanners, databases, and spreadsheet programs. For much of business today, technology drives information. Do not forget, however, that the paper and pencil can also be effective information tools. For a simple one-store retailer, information can be captured on paper, recorded on a ledger, stored in a file cabinet, and analyzed with a calculator. There's no need to invest in a high-tech solution when low-tech will do just fine.

I often tell my clients that data represents the "what," as in "what happened?" But these facts are worthless until you add the "so what?" (Why should I care?) and the "now what?" (What should I do about it?). That's when data turns into actionable information. We say every piece of data should be couched in terms of "what," "so what," and "now what?"

This frame of reference is particularly important when talking to customers. There is a tendency to drown customers in data. But like everyone else, customers don't have time to "connect the dots." They don't want to interpret your data, and even if they did, they may not draw the right conclusions or make the right buying decisions. Today's successful companies present information in a way that clearly outlines why it's important and what the customer should do about it. Some call this approach solution selling.

Let's look at a simple example of applying the "what," "so what," and "now what?" concept to a restaurant that one day decided to look at its non-food costs and noticed a significant difference in hand soap consumption over the past year.

> **What:** *"Hand soap consumption is down fifty percent versus last year."*

There are several potential inferences that can be drawn from this fact, this piece of raw data. A restaurant manager focused solely on costs may conclude that this is a good thing. After all, it saved money, right? However, the more important implication is:

> **So What:** *"The restaurant does not meet the minimum standards for employee hygiene set by the health department."*

Oops – not good! Saving money at the expense of customers' safety is never good for business. So what should the manager do about it?

> **Now What:** *"Retrain employees to use proper hand washing technique and monitor compliance closely for the next three months."*

Smart hand soap salespersons understand the full implications of that simple data point. They would not send the customer a message saying his soap purchases are down 50 percent in the hopes of getting an order. They would tell the customer that his hand soap purchases are down 50 percent and that his restaurant is likely out of compliance with local health codes. They would offer to come in and train employees in proper hygiene procedures to minimize the restaurateur's risk and promise to monitor future purchases to ensure employee compliance. Using "what," "so what," and "now what," the salesperson has taken a raw data point and processed it to produce information that is then used to solve a potential customer problem – and also capture a continuing stream of soap sales.

Information tools need to be chosen so that you can first collect useful data, store it, and then organize it so that discernable trends and patterns can become visible. People then need to take these conclusions and use them to create customer solutions. Don't just look to amass and retain data with your tools; instead strive to convert it so that your people can make intelligent decisions that serve the market.

COMMUNICATION TOOLS

Communication begins with the strategy itself. We've already noted in this book's introductory chapter that the vast majority of organizations don't broadly communicate their strategy to their employees. Many employees are left to infer their company's strategy from public advertisements and media reports. And the companies that do communicate it do so in vague or complex terms that leaves the employee wondering "so what? What does that really have to do with the way I do my job?" If your employees don't understand the strategy or don't understand their role in fulfilling the strategy, you're not likely to get the alignment you need across the organization that is necessary for consistent marketplace implementation. There are a number of tools a CEO can use to communicate the strategy: personal presentations and messages, internal newsletters, posters, success stories that celebrate the right employee behaviors, even the questions he asks the people around him (which demonstrates what he truly cares about).

But the need for communication and workable communication tools goes far deeper than just communicating the strategy. Communication is the oil that keeps the organizational engine running.

Some common communication tools are listed below:

- Internal tools (e.g. reports, business plans, capital request forms, e-mail, meetings, phone, voicemail, performance appraisals)
- External customer tools (e.g. product brochures, invoices, statements, advertising, sales presentations, business cards, reports)

Technology has both enhanced and destroyed corporate communication. In recent decades we've seen countless new and innovative communication tools that have resulted in a dramatic increase in the *quantity* of communications at the expense of the *quality* of the communications.

We've discussed aligning communications to the strategy and the need to be cognizant of the messages implicit in organizational systems and actions. Organizations also need to be aware of how they are using popular communication tools. Maybe you are making an internal presentation to management with PowerPoint or note cards, or you are disseminating marketing and sales material to external customers via brochures or in conjunction with a website. Regardless of the tool you use to deliver your message internally or externally, you must keep some important communication basics in mind.

Consider the following elements when analyzing all communications:

- **Goal**: Is there a specific goal/objective in mind? What do you want to happen because of the communication (what actions or decisions need to occur)? Who in the organization needs to act? What do you want the customer to do (buy the product, ask a sales representative, research the company on the web)? Make the desired end result crystal clear.

- **Distribution:** Who will receive the message and in what format (is the message catered to the specific audience's needs)? Are you using the appropriate vocabulary? Is the level of detail (facts, statistics, anecdotes) appropriate? How about the tone – is it the right one for the recipient (e.g. friendly and caring for the external market or efficient and straightforward for internal operations)?

- **Level of Importance:** What is the priority of the message in relation to other messages the audience will receive? Choose the appropriate medium, channel, and source of the message to match its priority level.

- **Timing:** When do you need to reach your audience? Think about when your audience will actually receive the information and when they will be able to take action. Schedule the communication to account for the time of its delivery (the date, holidays, and vacations, etc.).

- **Consistency:** Have you ensured that both internal and external communications match the marketplace strategy (and each other)? Actively work to root out contradictory or confusing information.

By taking the time to review your message for the above elements (and fostering this behavior in others), you can eliminate a lot of the noise that disrupts internal operations. You will also ensure that your customers are getting the right amount of accurate information, when they need it.

E-MAIL

Using e-mail has become so ingrained in the business world that it warrants discussion of its use as a valid communication tool (yes, I said valid). I emphasize this point because every client I work with at every level of an organization complains about the sheer volume of e-mail they have to wade through. Many complain the e-mail tool has now practically become useless because responses from coworkers to their e-mails are often delayed or never come at all. Other executives and managers tell me that they are a slave to their e-mail. I personally see people responding to e-mail during meetings, not because what they are addressing is more pressing than the meeting itself, but because if they don't keep up they'll fall hopelessly behind. A simple two-day business trip without e-mail access can result in two to three hundred messages waiting upon return. One of my clients even has a function built into his e-mail system affectionately called "e-mail jail." When an employee's e-mail inbox fills beyond a maximum memory level, the system automatically freezes the user's ability to send mail until the inbox is cleared out. Thus communications, no matter how critical, are halted until the employee sifts through scads of messages, many of which are trivial or unnecessary.

Why has the e-mail situation become so bad? E-mail functionality has made it far too easy to include everyone on even the most minor communications. Some of this behavior is motivated by the age-old desire to cover one's ass. Much of it is driven by the ever-increasing complexity of organizations and their work processes.

Beyond creating complexity from sheer volume, e-mail strips away some of the most essential human elements of communication (i.e. the non-verbal part). Instead readers are left to infer those cues and will often interpret your e-mail through their own personal filters, which sometimes adds unintended subtext. Direct face-to-face communication can be easily misinterpreted – phone conversations even more so. With e-mail, it's almost a guaranteed result. The more non-text cues we remove from a communication, the more likely it is to be misread and create problems for both the message sender and receiver. If a message has a high probability of being incorrectly interpreted, choose another medium outright or choose a parallel method (follow up with a call, a later meeting, etc.).

Despite its shortcomings, a good tool is still a good tool when used properly. Even though e-mail has been abused extensively of late, it still retains the following advantages:

- Affords convenience.
- Reaches geographically dispersed individuals (cost-effectively).
- Provides a written record for retention and referral.
- Allows users to plan, organize, and structure their thoughts before dissemination.

The key is to educate yourself about e-mail's limits and common misuses. If, for example, there is broad or regular information that whole departments or teams need to know, don't use e-mail. Place the topics on a shared database, intranet folder, or internal website. Provide one definitive source and reinforce everyone accessing that source for sharing group information. Those who truly want the information will know how to get it. Eliminate unnecessary noise by using the right communication tool.

MEETINGS

Meetings are still the backbone of most business operations, and just like e-mail, they merit further investigation. Like any other improperly used tool, many meetings are poorly managed, disorganized, or at worst time-wasting and demotivating. Used correctly, however, meetings can be turned into a more formalized tool for effectively managing a business, department, issue, etc. As a key element of formalized communication processes and tools, the simple meeting can yield incredibly positive results.

When I suggest a formal team meeting as an appropriate ongoing communication tool, I help the team develop the norms and rules of engagement for their meetings. A meeting is of no value if people are going to meet each week, discuss a bunch of nice to know stuff, and then go back to work. What has that meeting accomplished? Instead, I preach to my clients the 3-D Model: Discuss, Debate, and Decide. This simple model allows an issue to land on the table for discussion and get as many facts out as possible. The group is then allowed to debate the issue, each person having an opportunity to express his or her opinion. A decision is then made based on the rules of engagement the team has established. People see that they are being heard and that actions will be taken with accountability assigned. Repeating the process on a weekly basis further emphasizes the advantages. That's how meetings can be made into a more useful tool that drives the organization forward.

The three steps to conducting a 3-D Meeting are as follows:

1) **Discuss the issue (get the facts out):** Get out the relevant details and organize them to accurately depict the situation.

2) **Debate alternatives (express opinions):** Let everyone voice their perspective and collect possible courses of action (remember the customer's viewpoint).

3) **Decide on an action (using established rules):** Use whatever method of decision-making the team has pre-agreed upon, but act on the situation based on the discussion.

Meetings will also work much better if you plan ahead of time and develop standards or rules for the following commonly occurring questions/items:

- How will the meeting topics be prioritized to match time with importance?
- How will disputes over crucial facts be resolved?
- How will missing or inconclusive information be handled?
- How will time for everyone to voice concerns, opinions, and solutions be allotted?
- How will the final decision(s) be made?

Take minutes and notes during your meetings, as well. Assign a note-taker beforehand and make that individual responsible for circulating the minutes within twenty-four hours of the meeting. In the notes, record decisions and assign responsible parties to the deadlines for agreed upon actions (foster accountability). Also (because it does happen), decide how discrepancies or perceived errors within the minutes can be reported and addressed quickly and decisively.

Why go to all this effort? Regular standing 3-D meetings have several advantages. Among them are the following:

- Information is heard at one time by all meeting attendees.
- Thoughtful preparation for discussion topics becomes the norm (people do their homework knowing they will be debating their points and that a decision is pending).
- Issues are brought into the open before they become crises (better to let the team discuss and decide rather than take no action individually).
- Commitment to getting things done is instilled (people discuss then take action to drive progress).
- Members focus on the organization as a whole rather than just their specific area.

The 3-D meeting discipline can be applied at all levels of the organization and address any and all business situations. Time is a universally precious commodity in today's working environment. Employees want to know that participation in a meeting will enable them to accomplish their individual tasks and move their organization as a whole forward. The goal is to get people talking regularly and then to take that next step of making decisions and performing actions.

BETTING ON THE RIGHT CUSTOMERS

In 2003, Gary Loveman, CEO of Harrah's Entertainment, Inc., now the world's largest gaming company, offered us an inside look at Harrah's casino operations. His article, *Diamonds in the Data Mine*, published in the Harvard Business Review, highlighted how existing and new tools can be used to drive successful marketplace implementation of a differentiating business strategy.

In Gary's own words:

"We've increased customer loyalty, even in the current challenging economy, in two ways. First, we use database marketing and decision-science-based analytical tools to widen the gap between us and casino operators who base their customer incentives more on intuition than evidence. Second, we deliver the great service that consumers demand. In short, we've come out on top in the casino wars by mining our customer data deeply, running marketing experiments, and using the results to develop and implement finely tuned marketing and service-delivery strategies that keep our customers coming back."

The Harrah's story actually began in the 1990s, when then CEO Phil Satre expanded Harrah's from four casinos in two states to twenty-six properties across the country. More importantly, while most casino operators were building big, glitzy entertainment extravaganzas, Satre concentrated his efforts on his customers' love of gaming, specifically slot machines. He believed that cultivating lasting relationships with his core customers – slot players – would ultimately drive profitable growth. Thus the decision was made to invest in the technology necessary to collect and analyze data about these customers. These tools would be critical in transforming Harrah's from *"an operations-driven company that viewed each casino as a stand-alone business into a marketing-driven company that built customer loyalty to all Harrah's properties."*

By the time Loveman arrived in 1998, Harrah's had tracked millions of individual transactions and assembled a vast amount of data on customer preferences. Harrah's learned that its best customers were still only spending 36% of their gaming dollars at Harrah's. Thus there was tremendous upside. Loveman had to figure out how to change the customers' decision process so that they chose to spend more of their gaming dollars at Harrah's.

Harrah's used its information tools to guide its marketing strategy. The company found that 26% of its gambling customers accounted for 82% of its revenues...not a surprise to students of the 80:20 rule. What **was** surprising was who these people were. They weren't the flashy Las Vegas "whales" that every casino sought to attract. They were regular folks...former teachers, doctors, bankers, and machinists – middle-aged and senior adults with discretionary time and income who enjoyed playing slot machines. They didn't always stay at the hotel but typically stopped in on the weekends or on their way home from work. Using leading-edge predictive modeling, Harrah's was able to forecast the long-term value of a customer based on his or her playing habits. This innovation led to a breakthrough in strategic thinking. Instead of focusing on how much people spent in its casinos during a single visit, Harrah's chose to focus on their potential worth over time.

Harrah's chose to leverage its customers' innate desire for achievement by segregating them into three tiers: Gold, Platinum, and Diamond cardholders. Much like airline frequent fliers, Platinum and Diamond cardholders received greater levels of service that added to the inspirational nature of the program. For example, Harrah's created different check-in lines and processes for each of the three tiers. Every customer clearly saw the differentiating benefits (less time waiting in line) of achieving Platinum or Diamond status.

Harrah's also set up a series of triggers in the database. If, for example, the company discovered that a customer who typically spent $1,000 per month at Harrah's hadn't visited in three months, a letter or telephone call would invite him or her back. Harrah's telemarketers were trained to listen for specific cues and track responses to different offers. A certain percentage of customers responded to offers of a steak dinner while others were more intrigued by offers of two free nights in the hotel.

All of this information was entered into an ever-increasing database of customers and their preferences. The database capabilities were expanded to combine data from all of Harrah's properties, so customers could use their reward cards (and be rewarded) in multiple locations. In fact, combining the transactional data across all of its sites was so cutting-edge at the time that Harrah's developed and ultimately patented custom technology tools to do it.

The company's analytical capabilities grew right along with its database. Eventually it was able to identify which specific customers were playing at particular slots in Harrah's Las Vegas and what it was about that specific machine that appealed to them. This knowledge allowed Harrah's to configure the casino floor with a mixture of slot machines that benefited both the customers and the company.

Today, Harrah's owns, operates, and/or manages about 50 casinos. It still derives almost 70% of its revenues from gambling (as opposed to lodging, restaurants, shopping, and other entertainments). This rabid focus on its core business has given the company deeper insight into the preferences and characteristics of casino players than any of its competitors. While many casinos have attempted to copy Harrah's marketing approach and specific programs, their continued focus on facilities, not customers, has limited their success. As Loveman says, "We maintain our competitive advantage by using our human capital and technology systems to get to know our customers better."

So while its neighbors lure tourists with knights on horseback, fiery volcanoes, pirate ships, and mini-Manhattans, Harrahís will just keep refining what itís already pretty good at: leveraging its information and communication tools to ensure its regular customers are more than satisfied.

CONCLUSION

Your organization has picked a strategy for the marketplace. It has reviewed and aligned its processes with that strategy. Systems and structure have been brought in line to ensure the processes get done. People that will champion the processes have been recruited, educated, and exposed to the customer culture. Now take the final step and give people the right tools to execute the plans and processes. Ensure task tools enable a process step to be optimally completed. Employ information tools that drive through the "what?" and "so what?" of data to enable people to create "now what?" solutions. Thoughtfully apply communication tools properly in order to disseminate messages of value, coordinate resources, and reduce useless "noise."

Your tools need to serve your people, not hinder them. They need to enable consistent delivery of your unique marketplace promise. Make the choice of what tools to use based on rational and logical explorations of the outcomes they produce. Tools do not necessarily mean higher levels of technology. More technology *may* result in tools that produce faster results and have more features or better packaging, but is that what your customer wants? Is that in alignment with the image you hope to create? Use the best tool for the job at hand, the tool that adds value your customer (or end user) specifically wants and provides it in the most effective and efficient manner. That's simply good business.

BRINGING IT ALL TOGETHER – A CASE STUDY

*A*uthor's Note: The Strategy Activation process is not a theoretical construct. Over the past several years I have used this process to help my clients, large and small, improve their marketplace implementation. Whether retooling a division, remaking an entire organization, or integrating acquisitions, the process works. Throughout this book I've used examples without mentioning specific clients by name. That's because the nature of my work demands that I protect my client's confidentiality. I do this for two primary reasons:

1) *Even though very few organizations are truly proficient at marketplace implementation, nobody wants to publicly admit this deficiency.*

2) *The strategies employed and the successful implementations thereof often create real competitive advantage for my clients and they don't want their competitors exposed to the source of their newfound secrets of success.*

3) *The clients' needs always come first. Therefore, I have crafted the model case study below with specific details in the narrative altered to protect consultant/client confidentiality. The scenario depicted here and its key*

aspects represent a consolidation of my work on projects performed across multiple clients in various industries. PayRollers, Inc., the organization depicted, and the people represented are completely fictional.

PAYROLLERS, INC.

It was four years ago when Pete Green accepted the chief operating officer (COO) position at PayRollers, Inc. The company, headquartered in Denver, started out in 1984 as a local payroll services firm providing paycheck processing and employment tax filing services to mid-size firms in Colorado. From these humble beginnings, PayRollers had grown into a diversified human resources management firm with almost $600 million in sales spread over the western half of the United States.

Like many of its competitors, PayRollers grew through acquisition. Building from its successful base of payroll services, PayRollers expanded into a number of related services including 401(k) retirement services, expense management, time and labor management, benefit administration, and screening/selection services. This expansion enabled PayRollers to leverage its existing relationships with its clients' finance and human resource functions to capture an ever-increasing share of their outsourcing expenditures.

Having previously spent eight years at IKON Office Solutions, Pete was painfully aware that merely assembling a group of related services under a single umbrella does not a successful company make. In the mid 1990s IKON was primarily focused on office products and paper distribution in the United States and Europe. In 1995 it acquired the UK-based copier distribution and service company Southern Business Group PLC. This began a torrid pace of acquisition aimed at consolidating the business equipment sales/service industry and creating an integrated document management solutions organization. Between 1996 and 1998, after spinning off the paper distribution business, IKON acquired a staggering 220 companies.

This acquisition pace turned out to be too much for the firm and profits tumbled in 1997. Revenue peaked at $5.5 billion in 1998, but restructuring costs had resulted in a net loss. While the company returned to profitability in 1999, revenue continued to slide. Pete left the company as it became increasingly involved in paring back unprofitable and off-strategy operating units, many acquired only a few short years ago.

As general manager of the copier division, Pete experienced firsthand the challenges of integrating a large number of operations into his own division as well as failed attempts to attract copier customers to newly acquired related businesses such as capital leasing, coffee vending, and e-business software. He learned some hard lessons about the value of organizational alignment and the importance of creating business processes and tools that cut across business entities. Most importantly, he learned that to be one company, you must act like one company in the marketplace.

Pete was eager to bring his lessons to PayRollers. Unlike IKON, PayRollers had grown more slowly and was much more successful in integrating its acquisitions. Nonetheless, as PayRollers CEO Seth Thomas outlined in his conversations with Pete, something was still missing. The payroll services group continued to dominate PayRollers's business. PayRollers had been unsuccessful in generating the same customer acceptance for its other businesses. For example, only 22 percent of payroll services clients used its 401(k) services and only 9 percent of payroll services clients used its benefits management services. For some reason, clients didn't see the value of consolidating those services with a single vendor. Pete suspected he knew the reason why.

PayRollers was organized into service-specific divisions, many of them a result of the acquisitions that brought these expanded services to PayRollers. The five divisions were structured as follows:

- Payroll and Expense Management Services
- Retirement Services
- Time and Labor Management Services
- Benefit Administration Services
- Human Resource Services

Each division was run by a general manager who now reported to Pete. General Managers had complete P&L responsibility and operated their divisions as independent entities each with their own sales force, marketing department, customer service group, information technology team, and other necessary support functions. Rarely did the divisions share information with each other. In fact, Pete discovered that oftentimes the individual divisional sales people assigned to a common customer didn't even know each other. Pete believed that this discord was the main source of PayRollers's problems. The divisions went to market as separate companies, so they were subsequently treated like separate companies by their clients.

Rather than draw hasty conclusions, Pete did his homework. He spent the first six months in his new role learning every facet of PayRollers's separate businesses. He met with his general managers, read past research, rode with salespeople, and talked extensively with customers. The more he learned, the more he was convinced that PayRollers could improve customer penetration with a more integrated one-company approach.

In addition to learning all he could about his new operation, he also carefully studied his competition. In its dominant markets, PayRollers was, at best, a distant number three behind industry giants ADP and Paychex (numbers one and two respectively). Understanding how these two staked their claims in the marketplace was integral to developing a viable strategy.

With nearly $9 billion in global sales in 2006, ADP stood as the proverbial 800 lb. gorilla of the payroll/HR services industry. Even when counting only the $5.8 billion of revenue derived from employer services that competed directly with PayRollers, it was still three and a half times as large as Paychex. ADP served 545,000 clients and employed 32 million workers in 31 countries around the globe.

ADP attempted to align their service offerings to the needs of four distinct groups of customers:

- Small Business Services supporting businesses with fewer than 50 employees.
- Major Account Services supporting businesses with 50 to 999 employees.
- National Account Services supporting businesses with 1,000 or more employees.
- ES International Services supporting multinational clients outside the U.S.

Despite this segmentation, Pete found that ADP's customers skewed more toward the larger organizations. He surmised that this effect was a result of the company's high technology/low touch strategy. In its 2006 annual report, ADP boasted that it is *"one of the largest providers of computerized transaction processing and information-based business solutions."* Indeed, it had developed and/or acquired *the* leading-edge technologies available in the payroll services industry today. Its customers had access to everything they needed through intuitive and comprehensive web portals. Most inquiries could be handled quickly without requiring interaction with another human being. Additionally, ADP's databases interfaced seamlessly with its customer's accounting systems.

However, by relying on technology, ADP had removed the human element from its services. All customer service calls were routed to large, impersonal call centers. Issues or non-routine requests frequently required multiple contacts to resolve. Clients never connected to the same customer service representative twice; therefore, it often became necessary to explain problem details repeatedly at each new. This was a mild annoyance for large organizations that had ample finance and human resource personnel to manage their functions; but this approach did not work so well for small business owners with little time to constantly recap their specific situation with rotating frontline representatives.

The Paychex Corporation, in contrast, chose a high touch/low technology business model. Smaller customers (those with less than 50 employees) were assigned a local payroll specialist – a single point of contact – who worked closely with the customer week in and week out to process the payroll and to address questions or resolve issues. Client employee hours were phoned, faxed, or e-mailed to the payroll specialist, who then entered the data and processed the payroll. Paychex maintained a website offering its full range of payroll reports for those clients that wanted it, but they were primarily a person-to-person business.

For larger client organizations and/or technically savvy small business owners, Paychex offered software and online payroll management services. It was the collective opinion of most industry insiders that this solution wasn't nearly as comprehensive as the technology offered by ADP. When push came to shove, Paychex relied on its personalized service to differentiate itself from ADP.

Paychex served almost the exact same number of customers as ADP in 2006 – 543,000 – but generated only $1.7 billion in revenue. A simple calculation reveals that its revenue per customer was less than a third of ADP's, a sure indication that Paychex's customer base skewed more toward smaller companies. Pete concluded that ADP had successfully staked out the larger customer segment with a high technology strategy, while Paychex had successfully laid claim to smaller customers with a more personalized service strategy.

Like Kmart, caught in a no man's land between Wal-Mart and Target, Pete felt PayRollers occupied the middle ground between Paychex and ADP. PayRollers's technology was superior to Paychex, but not quite as sophisticated or scalable as ADP's. PayRollers's customers were able to access and interact with most of its services online, and its interface was considered to be fairly robust and intuitive. Due to this level of technology, PayRollers eschewed using its own personnel to perform manual data input. If a potential customer was unable or unwilling to submit information through the Internet, PayRollers simply walked away from that particular prospect.

At the same time, PayRollers was very sensitive to the personal side of the business and its salespeople were intimately involved with their customers. They were directly responsible for customer satisfaction and retention. If there was an issue or question, customers were directed to contact their respective sales representative. Over time, sales representatives had developed deep, personal relationships with their assigned customers, and often were perceived as the proverbial *"knight on white horse,"* riding in to save the day. Pete considered this aspect of the company's service to be a significant competitive advantage over the level of service offered by ADP.

It wasn't surprising then to find that PayRollers's client base tended to come from organizations occupying the middle of the company size spectrum. The firm attracted a loyal following among companies big enough to appreciate the capabilities of online data transmission but small enough that they didn't maintain the sizeable staffs able to chase down issues. These customers wanted a simple, technological interface to speed data input, but they also sought personalized, hassle-free issue resolution processes. These services were what PayRollers provided to the marketplace.

Kmart failed miserably in the middle. The question facing Pete was how to fortify PayRollers's mid-market position and begin to expand outward. In speaking with his customers and salespeople, Pete began to visualize a shift taking place in the needs of the marketplace. Customers at the lower end of the company size spectrum were becoming much more comfortable with technology. They were starting to see the time saving advantages of switching from paper ledgers to computer-based accounting. Time cards were being replaced with electronic time tracking. This shift in mindset favored PayRollers and ADP's emphasis on technology and electronic data transmission solutions.

At the upper ends of the company size spectrum, cost containment efforts were driving significant reductions in HR and finance staffs. Gone were the halcyon days when these functions had the personnel necessary to manage vendors and follow up on every issue. They now needed turnkey solutions that were easy to access and easy to manage. Responsibility, particularly in the area of issue resolution, was being pushed out to the vendors. The new mantra was *"Just fix it."* Managers had little time to manage vendors or deal with the problems they created. The winners in today's business climate were those vendors that could police themselves and make problems go away with little customer involvement.

Pete believed that PayRollers was well-positioned to exploit these opportunities. However, there were issues that first needed to be addressed. Customers told Pete that while PayRollers offered many of the numerous solutions they needed (payroll, tax compliance, 401(k), workers comp, etc.), each was sold and managed as an independent business, thus eliminating any potential benefit from vendor simplification. The same critique was true of PayRollers's web interfaces. Each division maintained its own technology; there was no consistency between them. Using more than one service required logging on to multiple sites with multiple passwords. There wasn't much advantage – if any at all – to clients consolidating all of their accounts with PayRollers.

Over the next few months, Pete worked with his general managers to develop a strategy that leveraged PayRollers's breadth of services and the market's desire for simplification. The marketplace promise they created was simple (no pun intended):

Compensation Simplification – rewarding your employees has never been so easy.

Supporting this promise were just two reasons to believe – two pillars:

1) One Face, One Place

PayRollers will approach the marketplace as one company providing clients with a single customer specialist – their own personal concierge for questions and issue resolution across PayRollers's entire service portfolio.

2) Seamless Information Integration

Customer and employee information will be integrated across service areas. Data will move across service systems without the need for customer intervention. Managers will access and input information through a single portal. Employees will have a single source for their personal information including timesheets, pay stubs, vacation usage, 401(k) status, and health benefit filings. They will also have access to general information including their employee handbook and the various policies associated with their benefit program.

All of the general managers agreed this was a big idea. While the one-company approach would require significant changes to the current organization, the customer benefits were spot on. Clearly this change would drive substantial growth at PayRollers through deeper customer penetration of the less-developed services as well as through the capture of new customers unhappy with their current vendors.

Pete and his team launched the strategy through a series of all-employee meetings. The strategy was very well-received. Employees started chanting, "*One Face, One Place, One Face, One Place.*" Within 30 days posters started popping up all over the building extolling the new mantra: *One Face, One Place!* Pete was thrilled, confident that they were on their way.

Unfortunately, after nine months the organization was no closer to bringing their new promise of simplification to market. The chants had died down almost completely. The messages on the posters seemed to fade into the background. It remained just business as usual in the individual divisions.

Undaunted, Pete held to the belief that the strategy could work. His customers had told him it would. They all wanted *compensation simplification*. They wanted to consolidate vendors and access all of their services through a single point of contact, a single system. The only problem was that Pete's organization couldn't figure out how to make it happen. There was no clear definition of what compensation simplification really meant, much less an understanding of how to implement it across the existing divisional silos. The organization needed help executing its promise before one of its competitors figured out how to do it first.

Pete was familiar with the some of the new work being done by IMPERATIVES, a company headquartered in Minneapolis. The firm characterized itself as a *Strategy Activation* firm. Pete had read about the processes its people employed. He knew that they helped companies like his bring their strategy to market by aligning their offerings, people, processes, and tools for consistent and successful implementation. He reached out to them for assistance.

Once contracted, IMPERATIVES's people spent the first thirty days immersing themselves in PayRollers's core businesses. They, of course, began with the requisite senior management interviews, but then they proceeded to delve much deeper into the organization to develop a general understanding of the business models and work processes of each operating division. They spent time with marketing, IT, finance, and sales management. They traveled with individual sales representatives and spoke directly with the customers. They listened in on the customer service calls and noted how issues were or were not resolved.

In general, IMPERATIVES's consultants learned that there was a basic understanding of and support for the new simplification strategy at the higher levels of management, but interpretations of how that strategy might affect existing business processes and service offerings differed greatly between middle managers. They also observed that employees at lower levels in the organization had firmly aligned their loyalties to their specific operating divisions; they gave very little thought to products, services, and customer experiences driven by other parts of the company.

During the next several months, the IMPERATIVES team worked with various groups at all organizational levels to guide the development of a common vision of what compensation simplification would really look like in the marketplace. It's easy to say, *"We want to provide our customers with simple solutions,"* but what does that really mean? How would PayRollers's target customers personally interpret its promise of simplicity? What products and services could consistently deliver on that definition of simplicity? This line of questions required PayRollers's managers to take a hard look at their existing products and services along with the infrastructure used to bring them to market. They had to ensure that everything they did, everything the customer experienced, reinforced and delivered the concept of compensation simplification. Anything short of that goal would result in just another unfulfilled business promise.

They started by examining the company's existing products and services in the context of the pillars supporting the strategy. Now Pete believed, based on his own research and investigations, that the way to deliver compensation simplification was to focus on just two pillars: *One Face, One Place* (integrated, one-company approach) and *Seamless Information Integration*. The first test of PayRollers's ability to implement this strategy was to determine whether it currently delivered its products and services through an integrated, seamless experience from the customer's viewpoint. Pete already knew this was not the case. Products were sold and delivered by each division – independent organizations with nothing in common but a corporate name.

Before an integrated solution could be developed internally, the company would have to get past traditional divisional thinking. People needed to think holistically. In short, they had to think like their customers. Their customers didn't care about PayRollers's corporate or organizational structures. They just wanted their needs met efficiently and effectively. IMPERATIVES used an exercise to categorize PayRollers's products and services the way that customers would categorize them, regardless of which of PayRollers's divisions managed them. The consultants created three buckets of services. A "payroll" bucket collected products from the payroll and expense management services, time and labor management services, and the human resource services divisions. A "benefits" bucket collected products from the retirement services, time and labor management services, and benefit administration services divisions. The third bucket, "HR management," catalogued the remaining services offered by the existing Human Resources Division. Products in each bucket were rigorously tested by PayRollers's managers against the promise of simplification. Those that passed made the cut. Those that did not were earmarked for enhancement or obsolescence. Product gaps were identified and new offerings were envisioned that further supported the promise of compensation simplification. As a result of these efforts, a vision of the products and services that would truly support the strategy emerged.

The summary of products and services that PayRollers developed for each pillar is shown in table 9.1.

Table 9.1 – Summary of Products and Services Vision by Pillar

One Face, One Place		
Payroll	Benefits	HR Management
One payroll solution that starts with time tracking for hourly employees, issues paychecks, submits state and federal tax deposits, and ensures compliance with all employment regulations, including workers compensation insurance.	One benefits source for all employee benefits including: – Health/Dental – Insurance – Life Insurance – Disability Insurance – 401(k) and/or pension – Legal Services – Affinity programs (i.e. mortgage discounts)	For smaller clients, a comprehensive database covering HR management tools and information from screening and selection to performance management to termination. Online access to the employee handbook (for larger clients). Online performance management system. Online salary review system. Employee master database system.

Seamless Information Integration		
Payroll	Benefits	HR Management
Easy data downloads to client financial system. TimeSaver time tracking system replaces timesheets and timecards. Data automatically feeds payroll. Online expense management facilitates submission and approval of all reimbursable employee expenses. Data automatically feeds payroll. A single web portal for managers to track the payroll process. Provides customized reports. Enables ad hoc queries to answer management and employee questions.	A single web portal for both employees and managers to track and manage benefits: – Track and approve vacations. – Monitor and manipulate 401(k) investments. – Investigate and clarify details of the various benefit programs. – Submit and track medical reimbursements. – Apply for additional programs and coverage.	Employee master database feeds: – Employee phone directory. – Employee records. – Information security clearances. – Federal and state reporting requirements. Performance management system feeds data to salary review system. All HR management functions accessed through a single portal.

While some of the work around products and services started to touch on the envisioned "experience" of doing business with PayRollers, the group still needed to push further. IMPERATIVES led the management team through a customer experience exercise. This particular exercise was intended to further show what it would be like for customers to do business with PayRollers in the future.

Working together, they identified four groups with primary customer touchpoints at client companies that needed to be considered:

– Finance Management

– Human Resources Management

– Employee Supervisors

– Employees

Each of these areas had a stake in PayRollers's offerings and performance. Each had a vote in determining if PayRollers lived up to the marketplace promise of compensation simplification. Thus, PayRollers needed to ensure that at each of these primary touchpoints it delivered compensation simplification via the pillars: either the *One Face, One Place* (i.e. one-company single point of contact) approach or the *Seamless Information Integration* approach. To drive the strategy, a matrix that envisioned the optimal delivery of each pillar at each touchpoint was created.

For finance and HR management, *One Face, One Place* now meant that they would have a single person assigned to the account as opposed to the four to five salespeople currently representing PayRollers's individual divisions. This person would be the customer's one go-to person for questions, issue resolution, and ongoing relationship management. The individual would be the customer's advocate within PayRollers, ensuring all commitments were met and actively identifying new and better ways to serve that particular customer's unique needs.

For the employee supervisors, *One Face, One Place* now meant that they would have a single online portal for all employee supervisory functions. Rather than the multiple systems developed and managed by each individual PayRollers division, there would be a single PayRollers system that enabled time card approvals, performance management, vacation tracking, and salary administration. System support would be available via instant online chat or a single 800 number.

Seamless Information integration now meant entering data into the system just once. Hourly clerical employees would enter their timesheets directly into the system online. Time clocks for hourly laborers would transmit punch in and punch out times directly into the system. Salaried employees would enter expense reports online. Supervisors would have access to all of these inputs for easy approval. Once approved, the data sets would feed directly into the payroll system for check processing. Once payroll was processed, the appropriate journal entries would be transmitted to the customer's accounting software for posting.

A summary of the key customer experience vision elements is shown in table 9.2 on next page.

Table 9.2 – Brief Summary of Key Customer Experience Vision Elements

One Face, One Place			
Finance Management	**HR Management**	**Employee Managers**	*Employees*
One person at PayRollers to manage the relationship. Consistent, effortless issue resolution. Continuous program re-evaluation for efficiency and cost savings.	One person at PayRollers to manage the relationship. Consistent, effortless issue resolution. Knowledge and expertise of industry trends applied to drive employee satisfaction, free management time, and reduce labor turnover.	Turnkey, intuitive solutions that minimize time spent managing people. All information necessary to manage their people available at the click of a button. Knowledgeable, personalized support available online or with a single phone call.	All information necessary to manage their lives at the company available at the click of a button. Turnkey medical benefits and reimbursement tracking. Knowledgeable, personalized support available with a single phone call.

Seamless Information Integration			
Finance Management	HR Management	Employee Managers	*Employees*
Individual systems (e.g. time tracking, expense tracking, payroll) feed data seamlessly through the process with little client intervention. Systems interface easily with customer accounting systems. Financial reports and management information available through a single, secure portal.	All the information necessary to drive the HR Management process is available to employee supervisors via a single portal (minimizing HR personnel involvement). Compliance and management reports as well as ad hoc query tools available through a single portal.	Complete employee records available in one place. New data entered becomes part of the permanent records available to all managers. Search tools enable easy identification and comparisons of candidates for promotions. Consistent application of performance management and salary review across the organization.	Real time access to timesheets, payroll accruals, YTD earnings, benefits programs, etc. Calculators for testing different W-4 assumptions, 401(k) assumptions, medical program choices, etc.

With the products, services, and customer experience fully envisioned, IMPERATIVES shifted its focus from the external needs of the marketplace to the inner workings of PayRollers. The goal was to determine the infrastructure enhancements necessary to deliver the now visualized services and experiences directly to the marketplace.

First it was necessary to figure out how to effectively breach the divisional silos within the company. Pete had no desire to toss away decades of institutional success by tearing down the existing divisional organization. That step would be too disruptive to the business and the customers it served. Furthermore, no matter what new structure replaced the existing one, silos would always have a tendency to redevelop. PayRollers instead needed to learn how to operate across its silos.

IMPERATIVES helped PayRollers see that the solution required the creation of a hybrid matrix organization (a mix of functional centralization and cross-divisional teams) that had both the skill and the desire to create and manage turnkey one-company solutions. The vision was to leverage the functional excellence of a centralized sales organization while retaining the product focus of the existing business divisions. That meant putting the right people in the appropriate jobs and rewarding them for the right behaviors. Ultimately, PayRollers agreed on the following key people needs:

- **A New Structure for Sales:** Sales will be centralized and support each division without any particular product bias or loyalty. Account managers will manage PayRollers's entire relationship with their assigned clients. As such, they will provide their customers a single point of contact for program development, program maintenance, and issue resolution. In a way, they become the "general contractor" of the customer relationship.

- **Dedicated Account Teams:** Marketing and operations experts from the existing divisions will surround the account manager. These individuals will bring their deep understanding of PayRollers's products and services. They will ensure that client commitments are feasible and delivered as promised. If the account manager is the general contractor, then the dedicated account team is comprised of the plumbers, electricians, carpenters, and masons that get the job done.

- **A Cross-Divisional Customer Service Team**: While the account managers will attend to the needs of the decision-makers purchasing PayRollers's services, a one face/one place single point of contact must support the supervisors and employees that will actually access and use the systems day to day. A new team of cross-trained customer service representatives (CSRs) will assume this role. These employees will have a broad understanding of PayRollers's products and services and the resources available to address customer issues. They will be the first line of personalized, one-company support. So instead of having the customer call an 800 number and negotiate a maze of voice response unit (VRU) questions, a live CSR will answer the phone, determine how best to assist the customer, and then properly transfer him or her to the appropriate resource.

- **One-Company Rewards**: The bonus structure for everyone from the chief operating officer down through middle management will be structured in a similar fashion. Existing division-based metrics and bonus plans will be replaced with customer-based rewards. The rewards will be carefully crafted to move loyalties away from divisions and functional silos and into alignment with effective implementation of the marketplace promise.

- **A Compensation Simplification Culture**: Public celebrations of implementation efforts that support the overarching strategy will reinforce the importance of the company's new direction. In both business and personnel reviews, managers will emphasize only those metrics that emphasize the desired marketplace behaviors. Promotions will be selected to reward those individuals that best exemplify the compensation simplification strategy.

At this point in the project, Pete had a vision of the differentiating products and services that PayRollers would offer in the marketplace and the internal organizational structure necessary to consistently deliver them. The final step was to visualize the work processes and tools that would enable his people to break down the silo barriers and provide the products, services, and experiences that would ultimately fulfill PayRollers's marketplace promise of compensation simplification.

Working with the IMPERATIVES team, Pete and his senior team created a long list of infrastructure modifications necessary to support the new vision. Some changes required minor tweaking of existing systems. Other, larger changes required broad-reaching, multi-phase IT projects. Using the Strategy Activation model as its guide, PayRollers concentrated on six areas:

1) Customer facing processes that include program development, selling, customer management, and issue resolution.

2) Horizontal workflow processes that govern the way work flows from function to function and division to division.

3) Vertical governance processes that establish organizational command and control.

4) Communication tools that break down silos and ensure that the right hand knows what the left hand is doing.

5) Information tools that link independent databases and enable easy customer information access and seamless operations.

6) Task tools that enable employees to perform their everyday tasks (e.g. sales collateral, job aids, handbooks, and resource directories).

This final step in the process resulted in a detailed Implementation Roadmap to guide development and bring the PayRoller's promise to market. To explore some of the projects outlined in the roadmap and how they were sequenced see Appendix A.

CASE QUESTIONS

Now that you've finished the case, please take the time to reflect on the questions listed below. Think about how a company like PayRollers would answer them (both before and after its transformation) and then think about how your own company would answer them.

1) Do you and your employees have a firm grasp of your organization's marketplace promise and the pillars that drive the delivery of that promise?

2) How do you know what your customer's expectations for your products or services are (what rational or systematic method have you employed to obtain this information)? Does your organization have its customer-facing processes mapped out so that you can simulate the customer's actual experience with your products or services? How would your customers rate the experience on a scale of one to five (five meaning it meets all their expectations)?

3) Do you have your metrics and rewards systems aligned with optimally performing the customer-facing processes?

Do you have any places where there is an inconsistency, where divisional loyalty takes precedence over serving the customer (If your answer is yes, how might this be addressed)?

4) Do the internal processes and tools you provide your employees match the competitive strategy your business is trying to execute? If you don't have the right tools, when will you obtain them? If you have the right tools but your people are still not able to execute, have you done the following:

- Identified the appropriate knowledge, skills, and abilities required by workers?
- Formally trained your people on proper processes and use of the tools?

5) Do the internal communications in your organization match the message to the customer so everyone is on the same page? Do your internal actions – compensation/reward systems, hiring/training/promotion practices, choice of tools/equipment – communicate support for the customer promise? If there is an inconsistency, why does it exist (hint: usually somebody is benefiting individually at the expense of the organization)?

6) How would your organization's employees respond today to a workplace survey asking them about the following areas in your company:

- Credibility – with customers and employees?
- Respect – for both customers and employees?
- Fairness – in how both customers and employees are treated?
- Pride – do employees have it? Does their work show it?
- Camaraderie (teamwork) – does it exist?

CHAPTER TEN

ANTICIPATING THE NEED FOR CHANGE

"Progress is impossible without change, and those
who cannot change their minds cannot change anything"
—George Bernard Shaw

S mall changes can alter our destination even as much as big ones. Consider the sea captain. He knows that there are many forces that control the movement of a giant ship in the open seas, especially in bad weather. He has to contend with the weight of the ship and the movement and mass of water along with the forces of the wind.

But he also knows that turning the relatively small rudder only a degree or two can alter the destination of a ship by as much as a thousand miles.

That's why a big part of this book is about the need for change – not only to thrive but to survive. If you don't change, you won't survive. We know that the vast majority of companies today don't implement strategy successfully in the marketplace. These companies need to change. Add to that the growing number of companies reacting to changing market conditions by introducing new strategies. These companies need to change as well.

STEPS TO SUCCESS: A RECAP

So change we must. That's what this book is all about. To illustrate that theme, let's recap the 10 top themes on Strategy

Activation and the changes those represent right here in the last chapter of our book:

1. Implementation: We must change with the knowledge that, while our strategies might be solid and effective ones, it will be the implementation of those strategies that dictates whether or not our new business strategies will succeed.

That's what the data tells us. In fact, nine out of ten business strategies fail in the marketplace. Not because they were bad strategies, but because they were poorly implemented.

What does poor implementation spring from? Let's have a look:

- Reasons for Implementation Failure:
- The strategy outstrips the capabilities of the organization to implement it.
- Employees don't understand the strategy or don't understand how to moderate their behavior to deliver the strategy.
- The organization's infrastructure can't support delivery of the strategy.
- Success metrics and employee rewards conflict with execution of the chosen strategy.

2. Creating a Promise: A marketplace strategy creates a promise. That promise may be leavened out in terms of mission, brand image, product positioning, value proposition, go-to-market strategy, or one of the other popular tools. Regardless of the vehicle, your promise tells the marketplace what you intend to deliver. As such it creates expectations in the minds of the customer who hear your message.

3. Going Beyond the Promise with Brand Pillars: The problem is that, more often than not, business promises go unfulfilled. This letdown has created an environment of customer cynicism. So to attract customers to your products and services, you need to go beyond the promise itself and provide clear reasons for them to believe that you can deliver on the promise made. These are often called pillars. They define HOW your organization will meet the expectations created by the promise. The pillars accomplish several things:

- They further define the promise for the customer, fine-tuning expectations.
- To the extent that the customer believes that your pillars fall within the capabilities of your organization, they add assurance that the company will make good on its promise.
- They provide direction internally for resource allocation, product development efforts, and system design.

4. Delivering on Your Promise: Once the strategy (promise + pillars) is finalized, we must align the organization to the consistent delivery of that promise in the marketplace. We need to address four key elements:

- Offerings that include your products and services and the customer experience of buying and using them.
- People that speak to organizational competencies, culture, and the methods by which we reward strategy-aligned behaviors
- Business processes, whether they be outward facing, guiding customer interactions, or internal, guiding workflow up, down, and across the organization.
- Enabling tools that support the completion of specific tasks.

5. Defining Customer Experiences: The economic emphasis on customer value has shifted from products to services to customer experiences. That's not to say that basic products and services no longer matter. It's just that they've become commoditized, easy to copy by competitors. Today there is little sustainable competitive differentiation in products or even services. The new battleground is the customer experience.

Quite simply, that overall experience is the sum total of all the little experiences the customer has with your organization, from the advertising messages to interaction with sales and customer service personnel to monthly billing statements. Each of these touchpoints creates an impression. These impressions, taken as a whole, create the image of what it's like doing business with your company and whether you've fulfilled the customer expectations created by the promise you made. At the end of the day, your products, your services, AND the experiences with your company must all reinforce the image you wish to create in the marketplace.

6. Motivating Your People: People drive organizations. If a marketplace promise is to be fulfilled, it is only because the employees believe it is important to do so and are compensated well for their efforts. It all boils down to three things:

- Do your people have the requisite skills to deliver the promise? The organization may have to move people around, retrain, or hire from the outside to prepare the organization to implement the strategy.
- Does your corporate culture align with the strategy? Do employees have the necessary values orientation to meet the specific needs of the customer?
- Are you measuring and rewarding employees for the right things? If you compensate employees for unaligned behaviors, your implementation will not be successful

7. Establishing Good Processes: A process is a collection of steps performed in sequence that eventually result in a finished product or service.

The output can be a product, service, or experience delivered to a customer, or it can be an internal input that enables another part of the organization to ultimately deliver on customer expectations in the marketplace. There are no inherently good or bad processes, only processes that are either aligned to or out of alignment with the company's chosen strategy.

The only way to know if your processes support your overarching strategy is to map and trace them, noting each step's effect on the overall customer experience and/or the organization's ability to fulfill its promises. Core processes must be examined and managed holistically across functional and divisional silos, the same way they are experienced by the marketplace.

8. Giving Your People the Right Tools: Your employees must have tools that enable, not hinder, their ability to accomplish their work in a manner consistent with your desired marketplace image.

These could be task tools that enable the completion of a task associated with a specific process step, information tools that provide critical information necessary to do one's job, or communication tools that ensure that everyone is on the same page of the playbook. As with processes, there are no good or bad tools, only appropriate tools. First, we must choose those tools that enable delivery of the promise we've made and the customer expectations it has created. Second, we must train our employees to properly use the tools and create the proper measurements to ensure they are being used correctly and consistently.

9. Back to Implementation: Successful marketplace implementation is hard. If it were easy, 90% of all strategies would succeed, not fail. It requires forethought, planning, and a relentless focus on the promise of your strategy. Strategy Activation is a discipline that can help a company prepare for flawless marketplace implementation. It's not an overnight fix. It's not a magic bullet. It's a recipe that takes time and careful attention to detail.

But the rewards – happy customers, energized employees, and a successful business – are worth every ounce of effort it demands.

10. Plan to Succeed: On the surface, the phrase "plan to succeed" sounds like a warmed-over Harvard Business School bromide.

But it's much more than that. To take the initiative to change, to sell that change to everyone in your company, to take the steps needed to make change work, and to share the credit when it does, are key points in a strategy activation blueprint for success.

Again, it's not easy to accomplish those things. There is a fine line between success and failure. In baseball, the difference between a .350 hitter and a .250 hitter is only a quarter-inch up or down the baseball bat.

But if you follow the steps outlined in this book and summarized in this final chapter, there's no reason you can't succeed and change the fortunes of your business in the process.

That's one success story that is just waiting to play out.

And only you can make it happen.

PAYROLLER, INC. IMPLEMENTATION ROADMAP

I n Chapter Nine I introduced you to Pete, COO of PayRollers, a mid-size payroll/HR services company at a crossroads. Pete's new strategic vision called for linking services across existing independent product-aligned divisions, thus going to market as a single company. This vision required significant change to the processes and systems that previously supported the organization.

Below is a summary of just a handful of the operational elements PayRollers will need to address:

- **Horizontal Process Approach:** Redefining each business process at PayRollers in the context of delivering a seamless customer experience. Process owners and process teams will be chartered to ensure that processes continue to flow logically across the various divisional and functional silos with the ultimate goal of fulfilling the marketplace promise. Processes and concerns that will need to be addressed include:

    - **Annual Planning Process**: Ensuring internal operating plans (divisional, functional) and customer plans align with each other and to the compensation simplification strategy.

    - **Data Management Process**: Maintaining data integrity as information moves across individual systems (e.g. the payroll process from time tracking to check disbursement to the customer accounting interface).

- **Information Security Process**: Protecting personal information. This process becomes a top priority as new portals are created with access to an ever-increasing number of systems.

- **Selling Approach and Process**: Retooling the way customer programs are developed (internally) and sold (externally). This adjustment becomes a necessity with account managers going from specialists to generalists.

- **Issue Resolution Process**: Developing new protocols and procedures that enable account managers and first line CSRs to quickly identify and solve customer problems.

- **Data Linkage Automation:** Providing seamless data transfer between divisional systems. Rather than rewrite the legacy systems, we will create interfaces between the systems that filter and format the data so that the output of one system can be used as the inputs for the next system in the chain. The goal is to remove duplicate data input and/or customer intervention across systems.

- **Biometric Time Tracking:** Replacing current timecard systems with digital fingerprint readers. This system will collect data in a form that will easily interface with existing payroll systems and eliminate employee cheating.

- **Improved Expense Management System:** Developing or acquiring a system that enables individual employee entry of expenses, supervisor approval, reimbursement through payroll, and integration with customer accounting systems. The current system is only designed to reimburse expenses

through payroll and requires the customer's finance personnel to manually enter the expense totals themselves into the
company's payroll system..

- **Customer Information Bridge:** Building an intuitive,
front-end tool to access the existing databases facilitating
ad hoc queries and reports. The new selling approach and
the issue resolution process requirements call for an easily
accessed, single view of the customer. At present, customer
program information is spread across fourteen databases.

- **Customer Service Response System:** Connecting the new
first line CSRs to our existing customer service call centers.
The system should enable first line CSRs to quickly identify
customers and access a complete customer history. When
the first line CSR is ready to transfer a call, the system will
enable a brief conversation between the transferring first
line CSR and the divisional CSR taking the handoff that
introduces the customer and the issue as it has been identified. The customer's information and history will then follow
the call. This step will prevent the customer from having to
repeat information after transfers.

- **Expanded Information Portals:** Linking the existing
portals into a series of single access portals to support the
various customer constituencies. These linkages will be trans-
parent to the customer. At this time our existing portals are
fairly robust, but each division maintains their own version
requiring multiple access points for customer managers and
their employees.

The required linked portals are listed below:

  - **Finance Management**: Providing access to all financial reports and query tools.

- **HR Management**: Providing access to all personnel reports and query tools.
- **Supervisor's Portal**: Providing access to all employee supervisory reports, management calendars, approval requests, performance management programs, and salary administration processes. Online chat support will be made available.
- **Employee's Portal**: Providing access to all benefit program handbooks, policies and guidelines, expense reimbursement submissions, vacation requests, medical benefit reimbursement filings, 401(k) management, hourly time tracking, and W-4 revisions. Online chat support will be made available.

- **Sales Collateral:** Linking the various divisional service offerings to one-company, integrated customer solutions using new selling tools. Tools will include sell sheets, presentations, sales letters, and brochures.

Clearly this transformation wasn't something that would happen overnight. Nevertheless, happen it must. Pete was wholeheartedly convinced of that. While it is true that a journey of a thousand miles begins with a single step, knowing which first step to take is extremely important. Thus, the final phase of the IMPERATIVES project was to create an implementation roadmap. Pete and his team had already clearly articulated the following:

- A vision of the future products, services, and experiences that would differentiate them in the marketplace.
- The infrastructure elements – organization design, culture, processes, and tools – needed to enable consistent delivery of that vision.

The final step was to prioritize and sequence the changes that were to come. It was decided that PayRollers would concentrate first on those enhancements that would have the greatest positive impact on the customer, while ensuring that internal processes didn't lag so far behind that employees grew frustrated or were unable to deliver on the promise.

Working with each function and each division, IMPERATIVES helped PayRollers develop an aggressive yet pragmatic approach to moving towards marketplace implementation.

0-6 MONTHS

- Scope out business requirements for one-company information portals.
- Design a centralized sales organization concentrating on the roles and responsibilities at each level, the selling approach, and the internal workflow processes.
- Map out customer issue resolution processes clarifying protocols, roles, and responsibilities for the account managers and CSRs.
- Scope out business requirements for the customer service response system.
- Scope out business requirements for data integrity and automation.
- Scope out business requirements for the customer information bridge.

7-12 MONTHS

- Link existing web portals into one-company information portals.
- Scope out the requirements for online chat support.
- Create a *Tier 1* customer management group reporting directly to Pete. This group would have cross-divisional

sales responsibility for the top 16 customers. Dedicate divisional operations staff to support each account manager, effectively creating cross-functional, cross-divisional teams.

- Train a limited number of first line CSRs to support the top 16 customers. Implement the first elements of the customer service response system.
- Implement payroll process automation at *Tier 1* customers.
- Test the customer information bridge with *Tier 1* customer account managers.
- Scope out product requirements for the new expense management service.
- Scope out product requirements for the new biometric time tracking service.
- Develop new selling materials to support the one-company approach.

13-18 MONTHS

- Add 12 more customers to the *Tier 1* customer management group. This group now manages 38 percent of the company's revenue.
- Train and assign two account managers to hunting new elephants (i.e. big clients).
- Implement online chat support for the information portals.
- Expand the first line CSR team. Prepare for switchover to a single 800 number for use by all customers.
- Implement the final elements of the customer information bridge giving sales and marketing simplified access to all divisional databases and providing a single, integrated view of the customer.
- Finalize the new annual planning process.

- Design the new compensation and rewards guidelines.
- Roll out integrated benefits administration tools to *Tier 1* customers' supervisors and employees.
- Acquire new expense management capabilities. Link the system to existing service capabilities.

19-24 MONTHS

- Complete the transition to a centralized sales structure. The transition will be staggered across the remaining four groups (*Tier 2*, California, South, and North). The transition will include implementation of the new internal compensation structures, customer planning processes, revised performance management program, and a new compensation simplification newsletter.
- Roll out product and service improvements (currently limited to *Tier 1* customers) to the rest of the marketplace.
- Switch all customers over to the integrated 800 number supported by the fully functional customer service response system.
- Test the biometric time tracking at five *Tier 1* customers.
- Roll out the expense management system to *Tier* 1 customers.
- Roll out the new medical benefits submission and tracking capabilities into the employee portal.
- With the roadmap complete, Pete and his team knew where they were going and how they would get there. They were ready to begin their journey.

INDEX

ABOUT THE AUTHOR

With a real passion for implementation, Scott Glatstein has been helping companies turn their visions into marketplace success for over 25 years. Whether creating new businesses, transforming companies or opening new channels he helps his clients align their marketplace offerings, people and infrastructure to their chosen marketplace strategy. His simple, focused approach to strategy development and execution has helped both established and emerging companies leverage their resources and build sustainable sales and profit growth.

Prior to founding IMPERATIVES, Scott's successful corporate career spanned both large and small companies including consumer marketing leaders General Mills, Pillsbury and ConAgra. His diverse career path includes senior management positions in product marketing, trade marketing, field sales and general management. A posting as CEO of Pillsbury Brands Africa in Johannesburg, South Africa added international business development to his broad skill base.

Recognized as a pioneer of disciplined strategy implementation, Scott brings a holistic approach to business execution. With Strategy Activation® Scott has created a bold, new, technique linking strategic planning and marketplace implementation. This straightforward model has helped companies large and small, here and abroad, turn strategic intent into satisfied customers.

Scott received a Masters of Business Administration in Marketing and Finance from Indiana University. He received a Bachelor of Science in Biochemistry from Michigan State University.

sglatstein@imperativesllc.com   952-591-8936